M000189159

DEVELOPER MARKETING DOES NOT EXIST

The Authentic Guide to **Reach a Technical Audience**

ADAM DUVANDER

Printed in the United States of America
First Printing 2021
First Edition 2021

10 9 8 7 6 5 4 3 2 1
R526

For my father, who promised to read this book, even if he doesn't understand it

Access the
Developer Marketing Library

Get the most out of this book—and your developer marketing. Your purchase of *Developer Marketing Does Not Exist* gains you access to a library full of Developer Marketing resources that will help grow and connect with developers on their terms.

You want to attract, engage, inspire, and educate developers?

The *Developer Marketing Library* provides you with:

- Worksheets for audience clarity

- Checklists for content development

- Templates for well-structured technical content

Plus other tools to reach more developers.

Visit **everydeveloper.com/library**

Advanced Praise for
DEVELOPER MARKETING DOES NOT EXIST

Essential reading for tech marketers and founders building developer-focused businesses. Developer Marketing Does Not Exist is a comprehensive yet briskly paced playbook overflowing with practical advice. Adam's humor and enormous generosity of spirit shines through on every page, taking the reader deeper into the developer mindset than a hundred persona exercises could hope to achieve and placing empathy at the core of technical marketing.

Antony Falco
SaaS Startup Founder

Genuine value exchange and authenticity are what separates developer engagement from noise. If you knowingly or unknowingly waste dev time, it is difficult to recover. Adam covers mistakes to avoid and tips that work in his book, an important read for anyone who partners with and seeks alignment with software engineers.

Delyn Simons
Ecosystem GTM leader

Before building successful commercial businesses Netlify, Snyk, and LaunchDarkly all started by creating developer-centric educational resources. Adam's breadth of experience with technical content at SendGrid, Zapier, and many of Heavybit's portfolio companies means he's able to uncover and expose true value for a diverse group of developers. This is a must-read for any team with a bottom-up go-to-market.

Dana Oshiro
General Partner and GM, Heavybit

Adam has put in the 10,000 hours on developer marketing and it shows. He understands what motivates developers and how they make decisions when evaluating tools and technology. A must read.

Jimmy Jacobson
Codingscape

TABLE OF CONTENTS

INTRODUCTION

There is no Spoon

If you've ever spoken at a large conference, you're familiar with that nervous energy before you walk on stage. For me, this often surfaces as last minute, usually irrational fears. That's what happened on my first trip to South America.

After 14 hours of flights, I arrived in São Paulo from my home in Portland, Oregon. Nice guy that I am, I'd given myself an extra day to recover from jet lag. I spent it chugging coffee and tweaking slides. To orient myself, I practiced the short walk from my hotel to the convention center. My talk would start off a full day's summit, so I didn't want any reason to be late.

The next day, I arrived before a single attendee had entered the place. Still feeling drained, I drank more coffee and watched the stage crew test the lights. It was an impressive setup, and I was about an hour from being the center of its attention.

I took note of the translation booth—they'd have native speakers dubbing my talk into Brazilian Portuguese live. The language barrier hadn't concerned me at all. I knew to speak a little slower to give time for the translation. Maybe not every joke would hit perfectly, but I was confident they'd understand my message.

It was shortly after the sound crew put on my microphone and the room was full that it first occurred to me to question a piece of information central to the next 45 minutes and core to my entire intercontinental journey:

Will the audience understand my references to *The Matrix*?

The movie was nearly 20 years old at this point. It had spawned sequels, comic books, video games, and likely increased the sales of trench coats. The first slide after my talk title would introduce the first of several analogies to the film. Then I would invite them, like Morpheus to Neo, to join me in a new reality. This was not a passing reference; it was important that they got it.

I checked the event schedule. There would be a coffee break after my talk. Worst case, I would go a little over time as I explained the plot to a decades-old, dystopian science fiction flick in translated Portuguese. As I imagined myself dodging slow motion bullets in pantomime, the emcee started my introduction. I took a deep breath and walked out to the expectant audience.

Fig. 1 APIX Conference Before the Crowds Filed into the São Paulo Auditorium

Developer Marketing Does Not Exist

In *The Matrix*, Neo visits The Oracle, who helps people navigate the reality of their artificial world. While waiting to see the clairvoyant, he meets a young boy bending a spoon. Though this utensil appears to be solid metal, he is able to make it flexible using only his mind.

"There is no spoon," says the boy, referencing the simulation in which they live.

Developer marketing does not exist in the same way as the spoon isn't there. How you approach developers will determine whether the marketing is visible.

You aren't reading a marketing book to learn Buddhist philosophy from a 20th century movie. Despite the title of this book, you know developer marketing exists in your world. It's a part—or, perhaps, the entirety—of your job. Chances are you've done a lot to market to developers already. Some of it has probably even been

3

successful. Now you want to do more developer marketing and be more strategic about how you approach it.

Developers sniff out anything that smells like marketing. They are a tough audience, because they'll ridicule you if they sense inauthentic motives. Even when you have good intentions, you can come across otherwise.

Developers have high expectations and are extremely skeptical. For both of these reasons, a developer marketer's job is difficult. If you approach it with the typical tactics you've used on other audiences, it will not work. Perhaps you've experienced the spam complaints on your lifecycle emails, the one-time use addresses pasted into your lead forms, or the Twitter callouts over technical inaccuracies in a blog post about your latest feature.

Your marketing messages to developers should not feel like marketing. You need to find ways to promote your product without promotion. With hype comes skepticism. The best developer companies have an authentic developer tone, which starts with really understanding where they're coming from. Solve developer problems—help them get better—and you'll have perennial fans.

You can reach more developers if you shift away from seeing yourself as a marketer. Yes, that word may be in your title, but reframing toward education will help you find the mindset to attract a technical audience. Even if you're a career-long marketer, take at least a few moments every week to imagine yourself as a teacher. Don't hold back, either. Make yourself the best teacher you ever had; someone who meets their students where they are, guides them to higher knowledge, and challenges them to improve.

Share Knowledge, Not Features

Through the lens of education, "marketing" fades into the background. In its place, your messages will intrigue developers to click, to dig deeper. You aren't converting visitors to leads, you're enrolling them in your class. Each blog post, tutorial, guide, or other piece of content invites them to learn more. The next step could be another lesson or even a signup, as long as it feels natural.

When I was the editor of ProgrammableWeb, I covered technical product announcements. Companies would excitedly release an Application Programming Interface (API) for their product and want press coverage. These API companies would send me press releases and blog posts that often began with words I learned to despise: "We are proud to announce." The problem was these were focused on the company or product, rather than the developers who would use the product. In fact, it was my job to find the actual story within these navel-gazing releases.

Developer marketers should be finding and telling that story themselves. Your product announcements will become much more impactful when you're sharing knowledge, not features. So will everything else you publish. Become that fantastic teacher who finds in themselves the energy to produce a spark within each student.

It's easier to focus on the features. When your marketing is surface level, you can stop at communicating what something does, rather than unpacking why it matters. Any marketer knows that it's the benefits, not the features, that really resonate. With technical products, it's much harder to dig into the why topics. But it's necessary if you're going to reach more of the right developers.

What You'll Learn in This Book

My role here is to teach the teachers. Armed with the "there is no spoon" philosophy of developer marketing, you'll see how it's applied at some of the best developer companies. Even better, you will learn how to apply it in your own role, with your larger team, and collaboratively across your entire company (and beyond).

We'll start with the foundational importance of developer experience. There's no use attracting a bunch of developers to an API, tool, or other product that is missing the basic elements they have come to expect. You'll find 13 areas we've identified that make a great developer experience. When you get the experience right, you can apply the same approach to the rest of your marketing. Plus, your marketing will be more efficient and effective.

Three common types of developer content—blog posts, tutorials, and guides—each get their own chapter. You'll see how to use a developer-focused approach to make your content more successful. We'll look at the importance of an editorial calendar and treating your blog like a publication. I'll break down the structure of a tutorial, which will demystify this staple of documentation that can do double duty as a top-of-funnel attraction. Similarly, I'll describe guides, which some of you may call eBooks or whitepapers. This final content type may be the most different for developers than what most marketers are doing. It will likely leave you with a plan to shift gears, or at least experiment with a new perspective.

Getting any one of these three types of content right could make a major impact on your traffic, your product, and your business. But it's clearly not the entirety of your developer marketing.

One by one, this book goes through four common non-content strategies to attract developers: events, open source, free tools, and advertising. We cover the best practices of each, along with the missteps to avoid. At this point, you should not be surprised that you'll approach each of these channels with the same mindset as your content. Yes, even advertising can be about education over promotion.

Finally, we'll look at your developer marketing organization. The skills of a complete developer marketer may not exist in a single person. However, you can piece them together—with team members across your organization, as well as outside experts—to create a Dream Team that could even get Michael Jordan's attention, if he ever learns to code.

What You Won't Find in This Book

Don't expect regurgitated Marketing 101 fluff in these pages. There are better places to learn that and more qualified people to teach it. You won't find a single visual of a funnel, nor a deep discussion of each stage. Those certainly have their place, but not in a book that's asking you to see past marketing tactics to really connect with developers.

Similarly, I won't show you how to wire up your analytics system to track goals and trigger segmented messages. Again, these can be useful, necessary tools, but I assume you or your team have this knowledge. If you don't, you know where to find it. These measurements only really matter when you're performing the activities to produce the metrics. Those activities are the focus of this book.

彑

I wrote this book because I don't want to see more bad developer marketing. Long before I founded EveryDeveloper, I wrote code for a living. I felt many pains now solved by an industry of developer tools—and many more that still plague developers. More than once, I banged my head against terrible, awful documentation, only to discover it was outdated.

As a journalist at Wired, then the editor of the first API-focused publication, I worked with many marketers who were shouting irrelevant, tone-deaf messages at a technical audience. It wasn't sufficient for me to translate their meager attempts into news. Some melodies just can't be auto-tuned, at least not without going to the source.

Next, I worked in roles at a number of developer-focused companies, from small startups to large enterprises. With EveryDeveloper, my team and I have helped dozens of products like yours find the right audience of developers.

As a developer communicator, developer relations leader, and technical content expert, I've seen your product from all sides. I understand what it takes to get internal buy-in, how to form your angles around a high-level vision, and what the audience on the other end of your copy wants to see.

This book shares my knowledge, gathered over a decade of working with developer companies and a decade before working as a developer. It encapsulates the philosophy I use every day with clients at the best developer companies. The goal is to help you apply this approach so you can reach more of the right developers with authentic, resonant messages.

$$\not{\exists}$$

Back in Brazil, the title of this book was displayed across four giant screens in a cavernous auditorium. I started with an acknowledgment that it might seem awkward for a developer marketer to be speaking about his field like it doesn't exist. The chuckles in the audience helped me relax a little. At least the translation was working.

Now, for the important question: I raised my hand, the classic speaker technique that invites others to do the same. "Who here is familiar with the movie *The Matrix*?"

I paused for my English to be translated into Portuguese and broadcast to the United Nations-esque ear buds attached to every attendee's head. Then, the first signs of success: smiles, nods, and even a few brave hands raised. The Wachowskis' film had also made the journey to South America.

Relieved, I relayed the story of the spoon boy. I explained that developer marketing does not exist" because done well, it doesn't come across as marketing. Then I put up a slide of Morpheus' hands from *The Matrix*. In one was a red pill, which represented knowledge of the simulation in which they were living. The other, a blue pill, would maintain the facade.

I put my arms out to the audience and requested they do the same. Then I asked them, as I am asking you now, to take the red pill with me and explore a world where you question the typical marketing approach. Let's reach more of the right developers through education and support.

Let's understand their problems and help solve them, even if some of the developers won't use our products. In our work, let's share knowledge, not features.

Let's create a great developer experience and build trust with a valuable technical audience. The first chapter shows how you can assess and improve your experience today.

DEVELOPER EXPERIENCE

Prepare an Environment Where Developers Will Thrive

In the 1974 movie *Blazing Saddles*, a Western town hatches a plan to evade the bad guys. They recreate their entire town in the middle of nowhere in hopes of luring the antagonists into a trap. Rather than physically rebuild every structure in the town, they merely erect facades of each place. When viewing the town from Main Street, it seems like the real thing. However, behind each structure are boards leaning to keep it standing tall.

In this fake town of Rock Ridge, this simplistic approach worked. The townspeople planted booby traps and explosives. With the antagonist stunned, they were able to win the day.

Don't expect the same easy victories with developers. They will look behind the facade of a polished portal and want to see how your product works. The traps you set for them—even accidentally—will keep them from being successful with your API. Developer experience is not simply a well-designed site, though that can certainly help. It's the sum of every interaction a developer has with your company, from before they even discover your website through being a veteran customer, assuming they make it that far.

Attracting and converting developers requires that you give attention to how they experience your product. If you buy into the educational approach of "developer marketing," then the developer experience you provide is foundational. If you attract developers to your facade with platitudes and hype, it could easily provide a negative impact. Take the time to understand the elements of developer experience and where you can improve. Then, as you attract developers using the methods throughout this book, there will be something real behind the promises. You'll show not only that you understand them, but that you can really help them.

Far too often, developer experience is seen as the very first experience, which can equate it with a single onboarding task. To be successful, there's a much longer relationship you need to have with a developer. Some of the best developer companies have entire teams—or multiple teams—dedicated to developer experience. That's a long-term investment, which pays off over many, many developer interactions.

Don't mistake developer experience for just design, just onboarding, or just documentation. It's all of those things, plus more. Later in this chapter, I'll share the 13 elements of developer experience that we identified at EveryDeveloper. We use it to calculate a "Developer Experience Index" for our clients. This 1-10 rating helps them see how their experience measures up to the ideal and where they need to focus their efforts. Before we get into the details, it's important to consider the developer journey.

Fig. 2 Developer Journey from First Impression to Last Interaction

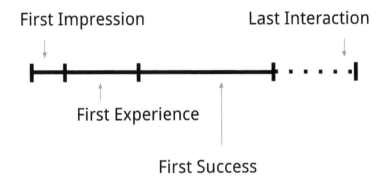

The first impression colors how a developer approaches your company. Next, once a developer has chosen to give you a shot comes that initial experience, the thing you might mistakenly call the developer experience. While getting started is important, it's only the start. You next need to help a developer become successful, which will give them a higher likelihood of becoming a customer. Finally, they'll still need a great ongoing developer experience. Their last visit—as in the most recent—becomes important.

First Impression: Discovery and Reputation

You will never control every aspect of a first impression. There may be actions you can take to push things in your favor. And, more importantly, you can get the things you do control in order.

As an analogy, let's consider the experience of watching a movie. The opening titles contribute to your first impression, as does the first scene of the film. Where you watch it also impacts that first impression: are you in a theater, in a dark room at home, or are you watching on your phone while your kids rage around you? Outside of the setting, who told you about the movie may determine whether or not you watch it at all. And certainly, word of mouth impacts how you interpret the rest of your first impres-sion.

There are many more aspects to how we feel about a movie in those first moments, but did you see how many on that list are things a filmmaker cannot even influence?

Word of mouth can determine whether or not a movie is successful. Similarly, how developers talk about you—on Twitter, in forums, and on the countless Slacks you'll never track—can make or break your first impression. Adopting something new into your developer stack is a big investment, initially and over time. It's a dependency that developers are reluctant to take on. Because of this hurdle, how other developers talk about you will be an amplified consideration.

Of course, the best thing you can do is create a great product, then back it up with a great developer experience. You can also help developers find out about you on their own.

A great method to reach more developers is through problem-focused content, using search engines to help developers find you. These important pieces of content get their own chapters throughout the book, but it's important to point out it's a rare first impression that you *can* control.

For example, let's say a developer wants to implement an efficient location search feature in their app. To do this, they realize they will need to index their database for geospatial searches. Without the proper database knowledge, they turn to a search engine. Surely someone in the past had this issue and already fixed it. They may find StackOverflow answers and other discussions. If one search result mentions your tool, that may make a good impression.

But what if they find your in-depth post showing them exactly how to add indices and some rough spots to avoid? Content like this can help developers discover you first and it goes a long way toward a positive first impression. At a minimum, you'll endear yourself and your brand to developers. And if you happen to have a geospatial database product, you might even gain a customer.

In order to make the problem-focused content approach work at scale, you'll need to keep topics focused on developer problems, not your particular solution. Some Search Engine Optimization (SEO) skills will help, too. When it works, it can be a powerful channel to orchestrate that first impression.

Beyond blogging and content, other areas you can control are your web properties themselves. Typically, this includes at least your primary website and a developer portal. Apply the "share knowledge, not features" mantra across every message to developers.

Your home page, if it is meant to reach developers, should speak to a technical problem. That doesn't mean it needs to get into the technical solution. For years, SendGrid's home page called out to developers with its promise to "Increase Email Deliverability." That message likely resonates with other personas, as well. When developers read it, they think of all the times they've been asked why people aren't getting emails. They've dug into code; they've fiddled with server settings. That simple home page message encourages them to dig in and discover a service that solves their problem with a simple API.

SendGrid (where I was among the first 100 or so employees) also has great word of mouth. Once developers discovered this great service, they told other developers experiencing email-related problems. No matter how warm the introduction, a developer is still within the first impression when they land on your website.

You still have a chance to affect their impression. And that goes beyond the promise on your home page.

One of the first things a developer will look for is your portal, documentation, or other signs of a section of the site specifically for them. Remember, that home page promise could appeal to marketers or product managers, too. Developers are looking for the technical details, which they know sits within your portal.

You would be surprised how difficult it is to find documentation within a company's navigation. Even when developers are a core audience, the link sometimes hides behind a dropdown or, worse, a euphemism like "partners." I like to play a game I call "find the API" where I see how quickly I can make my way from the home page to the portal. I don't always win.

Once they've found your portal, the first impression continues as they attempt to understand whether you really solve their problem. You can reiterate your home page promise here, perhaps with an even more technical bent that hints at your solution. Highlight common use cases and make it easy to discover your full reference. Most importantly, you want to usher them as quickly as possible into their first experience.

First Experience: Getting Started and Onboarding

If your developer portal could have only a single element on it, I would choose a big button that says, "Get Started." In fact, if you start with that design and build around it, you could be well on your way to a great first developer experience. Yet, a lot of things get thrown into that first page a new developer sees.

Fig. 3 This Developer Portal Makes Many Common Developer Experience Mistakes

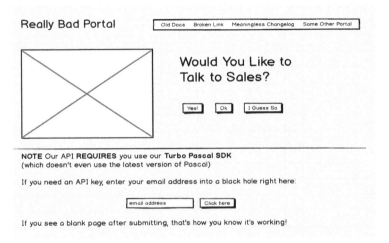

You want to avoid the bad portal that attempts to do too much or forces developers into your sales team's idea of their first experience. Instead, if you help them get a quick idea of how your product works, they're much more likely to sign up. They might even use their real email address!

Your getting started guide is the ultimate initial experience. Choose a common use case and walk a developer through what it takes to use your product to solve their problem. You can't cover everything with this guide, just the most important things to get started as quickly as possible. For a first experience, you want to decrease the "Time to Hello World," the gap between reading the document-ation and writing the first bit of code on their own machine.

Think about the experience right after you buy a new car. While it may have been preceded by frustrating negotiation, you're past that. Now you are about to drive your new car off the lot. Your salesperson hands you the keys, then walks you through the basics of operating the vehicle. They do not extract the thick manual from the glove box and flip through it one page at a time for hours. They simply give you the minimum amount of information you need to avoid a crash on your drive home—or perhaps just off the car lot, where a collision becomes your problem.

Your getting started experience should be the written form of the car walkthrough, written by someone who understands developers. The rest of your documentation is the manual in the glove box, and it can stay there for now. Developers know how to find it.

Avoid These Common Getting Started Mistakes

1. **Don't put your product first.** Yes, developers are getting started with your product, but the use case should still be front and center. Choose a common problem and show how to solve it with a subset of your full functionality.
2. **Don't include a bunch of concepts.** Sometimes there's context that you need to know before using your product. Don't front-load it within your getting started. Instead, drip out the concepts as needed during the first experience. You can always link to the full concepts documentation.
3. **Don't cover everything.** Remember the car salesperson doesn't walk you through the manual. Developers aren't looking for a lengthy guided tour. You should get them as quickly as possible to experiencing your product. That's it.
4. **Don't have multiple getting started guides.** You'll have many tutorials, and some may be introductory in nature. But there should be one initial experience, staking a clear claim of what you expect developers to do first. You might have different versions of the getting started guide for multiple languages, but you can guide them through a single place to make that selection.
5. **Don't go too long.** Since this is a first experience, you want it to be consumable in one sitting. So, keep it short. Once you've explained the minimum information needed to see the potential in your product, end the guide. You can always suggest some next steps at the end of the guide, with handy links for developers who are ready for more.

⨾

As developers get started, there's a natural opportunity to ask them to sign up for your product. If there is a free trial, evaluation version, or even forever free account you can offer, now would be the time to provide that offer. To keep the flow of the first experience, the signup should be self-serve and without delay or cost.

Of course, some developers will sign up before they read the getting started guide. You should have a similar experience for those developers. After signing up, you should have a meaningful onboarding process. Do not just drop them into an empty dashboard. Be mindful of how you handle that impression immediately post-signup. Taking a cue from the portal, you should have a single next step to suggest.

Often, that next step is to follow the getting started guide. You could also bake some of the concepts of the guide into your onboarding experience. You can walk them through creating a new project within the dashboard, or show how to add new data visually before suggesting the API option.

The same suggestions for getting started guides apply here. Your onboarding should not attempt to give a tour of every last feature or explain every concept that someone needs to know. You want to make the first experience positive, so they stick around for the real goal: using your product for a real project.

First Success: Use Cases and Sample Apps

Time to Hello World is an incredibly important part of developer experience. Your getting started guide, onboarding, and other content takes a developer from the hypothetical to the actual with your product. Until developers have the first experience, you're simply a tool that might help them. However, you don't want them to stop. They must take a next step (or multiple steps) to arrive at the first success.

Imagine you want to learn the piano and you've never touched a keyboard. A piano teacher might first show you how to find middle C and to play a simple scale starting with that note. That's the first experience, but you're a long way from playing a complete song. Your next step would be to learn a few chords, or a simple melody. That's where you'd first feel success, like you were on your way to learning piano.

For developer experience, the first success is when developers have something that feels like a complete app or integration. They might not deploy this first success to production, but it's an early version of something that could later be used.

The most important element of a first success is to understand how developers want to use your product. The more about specific use cases you can include in your developer experience, the more likely they'll be able to get to first success.

Sometimes there's resistance from marketers of robust technical platforms. There are many, many problems that can be solved with general tools like cloud compute, databases, and other infrastructure. The key is to seed a developer's imagination with common use cases so they can grow their own ideas. You aren't stifling creativity or limiting possibilities by sharing the ways others use your product. It's quite the opposite.

For new products or startups, exposing use cases is harder. You probably don't have a lot of examples to point to in production. However, the project was started, or the company founded upon at least a hunch—if not a bunch of proof—that the market needs your solution. Focus on those early problems you think are likely to be the most useful. Then create documentation and other content around those problems and your solutions.

To brainstorm a good list of use cases, consider some ways you might organize them:

- By industry
- By company size
- By customer segment
- By business department
- By type of developer (persona)

You may find a single approach can get you plenty of use cases to help direct developers, at least at first. For example, Twilio is able to provide a deep list of 10+ use cases for its communications platform by focusing on business departments, industries, and company types. Behind each of these use cases are one or more products to solve a specific problem within an organization.

Fig. 4 Twilio's Use Cases Organized in Three Categories

Twilio Solutions

Communications are transforming the digital customer journey
See what you can build with Twilio

Department	Industry	Segment
Customer service Offer personalized support at scale.	**Financial services** Engage clients with convenient and secure communications.	**Enterprise** Build exceptional experiences on every channel, anywhere in the world.
Marketing Deliver the right message at every step of the customer journey.	**Healthcare** Transform the way you care for patients.	**Nonprofit Organizations** Help more people with predictable business adoption.
Operations Increase efficiency with coordinated communications.	**Hospitality** Provide personalized guest communications.	**Startups** Scale up your startup and connect with more customers.
	Real estate Reach buyers and sellers when it matters most.	
	Retail Make every customer conversation count.	

Sample applications are a great way to both communicate a use case and give a developer a quick win to get them to first success. Someone internally may have already built these applications, such as developer relations or sales engineering teams. At startups, it's often founders and early employees "eating their own dog food." If you don't already have them, you'll need to build some samples. Encourage someone within the company to create a new example based on a known problem or look externally—a freelance developer or a member of your community may be interested, typically with compensation.

A great sample application will include:

- Full code needed to run the app
- Walkthrough tutorial explaining how it works
- GitHub repository that includes code and basic documentation

- Working demo to show how it looks when complete (optional)
- One click installation in cloud hosting, like with a Heroku button (optional)
- Case study of a customer who successfully runs something similar (optional)
- Interactive code explorer to pull in tutorial content while viewing the code (optional)

As you can see, many items are optional but can greatly improve the developer experience. That is, each of these items streamlines the effort needed to reach first success with a sample app. They remove the things every project needs and let the developer focus on what elements of your project are different than most. Plus, nobody likes copy-pasting code line by line or fighting with configuration settings to get a project in a shareable state.

You want developers to be able to easily take the next step with your product after their first success. They will either directly become customers or will act as champions for your product within their company. In both cases, a great experience—from first experience to first success—will help pave the way.

It may seem like developer experience should stop here. It's true that a developer who has integrated with your product long ago is unlikely to revisit the getting started guide and may not even touch another sample app. To ignore these users with your developer experience is a mistake.

Last Visit: API Reference and Support

Much of your documentation and content is focused on the early developer experience. You want to quickly introduce new developers to your product and help them be successful. Retaining developers with a great ongoing developer experience should also be a goal. Not only will that help the company by limiting churn, but it also increases the chance that these developers will sing your praises to their developer friends.

Many elements of your documentation can give a great ongoing developer experience. Primary among them is your complete reference. For a RESTful API, this means describing every HTTP method on every endpoint. You want to leave no detail to interpretation and no response to be discovered by experimentation.

For a REST API reference to be complete, it must include:

- Every endpoint and HTTP method combination
- Field names and types sent with each request
- Field names and types returned with each response
- Example request and response objects
- Potential and expected HTTP status codes
- Field names and types sent with error codes
- Error messages and their human-understandable meanings

As you can see, there's a lot that goes into a complete reference. In addition, you want to ensure that the reference is accurate, saving a developer from finding an issue where the docs don't match reality. Data formats like OpenAPI and JSON Schema can help your internal teams validate that actual usage matches what you expect.

Fig. 5 SendGrid REST API Reference

Further, you can use API description formats to generate some of your documentation. A modern API must have an accurate and updated API reference. Automation is the only way to know that's the case. Plus, you can make your OpenAPI document available publicly, which allows developers to better understand your API using their own tools.

Another piece of the ongoing developer experience you should consider automating is the Software Developer Kit (SDK), a wrapper library to help access your APIs. You'll want to provide an SDK for each programming language that is popular with your developers. The SDK becomes the true interface for a developer, which helps them build faster. The best developer companies may have support for six or more languages. You can generate these libraries with companies like APIMatic (whom I advise) and open source software like Swagger CodeGen.

You may still want experts in each language on your team (or available as freelancers) to build sample applications and other examples in each of your supported languages. These team members can also be made available to answer developers' technical questions. Just as interpreters help communicate between spoken languages, this team (often called developer advocates) can translate between code a developer expects to write and what is required by your product.

Indeed, support is an important part of the ongoing developer experience. Developers should be able to see that humans are behind your product. One easy way to do this is to make it easy to ask a question. Add an email widget to your portal, dashboard, and documentation pages. Upgrade that to a chat widget only if you are ready to staff the chat with people who can answer the questions. Developers want to know there's someone available, but their trust will be eroded if that someone doesn't have the knowledge they expect.

Even better is to provide proactive outreach and support. This is especially true of existing customers. Find out their frustrations through feedback widgets and personalized emails. Then work to fix those issues in your product or documentation. You can even review product usage on an individual level to discover issues you can help fix. For example, if a customer consistently receives a high level of a certain error, a proactive offer to help solve the error may make a fan for life.

Finally, how your product or API is designed is an element central to the entire developer experience. You'll find many books covering those topics and you'll want to build your developer product with best practices in mind. The good news is you will find out where you've missed the mark when you adopt the principles of a great developer experience. Most of them have been covered in the developer journey pages you've just read. In the next section, you'll find all 13 areas that EveryDeveloper analyzes enumerated and prioritized.

Elements of a Great Developer Experience

A great developer experience is not a clean design or flashy features. When a developer really uses your product, you won't be able to hide behind a facade. That sort of thing only works in the movies. You want your developer experience to improve every interaction a developer has with your company, from the first impression to the most recent API call or visit to your site.

For five years, EveryDeveloper has analyzed the developer experience of APIs and other tools. Before that, I saw thousands of APIs as the first editor of ProgrammableWeb. Using that background, I created the DX Index, a rating system for developer documentation and websites. Using the 13 criteria in this section, I generate a 1-10 rating.

You can self-assess your DX Index with a short quiz at dxquiz.com.

1. Libraries in popular languages

A lot of a developer's experience with an API comes through code. When you provide SDKs, wrappers, or libraries across multiple languages, you are more likely to cover the ones developers use. Language-specific libraries help at every stage of the developer journey: they see, upon first impression, that you speak their language; they are more likely to get started faster because the library can be easily imported into their tools; you can provide sample apps built atop the libraries to help them reach first success; and when you update SDKs alongside the APIs, it provides a great ongoing developer experience.

Since libraries in popular languages are very important to developers, it is weighted at the highest level in the DX Index.

2. In-depth getting started guides

Your getting started guide provides just enough information to give an initial taste of your product. At the same time, you want enough depth that it provides a useful introduction to what is possible. It should not cover everything, nor should it demand an academic study of your company's concepts. Provide what's needed to get a developer to Hello World, so they can clearly see (and understand) the next step.

Since getting started is very important to the initial developer experience, it is weighted at the highest level in the DX Index.

3. A self-serve option

Some companies see sales as a speed bump that separates the serious prospects from the tire-kickers. Developers see it as more than a speed bump; it's a blocked road—and they *want* to kick the tires. That's how developers understand things. Provide a self-serve option, in whatever way you can, so that developers get a chance to check out your product for themselves without first having a conversation.

Since self-service is very important to developers who feel delayed by sales tactics, it is weighted at the highest level in the DX Index.

4. A clear pricing page

Related to self-service, developers don't want any gotchas. Salespeople provide gotchas, which is why developers want to be able to sign up on their own. Similarly, "call us" and other hazy pricing practices make developers nervous and skeptical. They need to know whether they're in the ballpark before they give your product a try.

Since a developer needs to understand the pricing structure before moving forward, it is weighted at the highest level in the DX Index.

5. A free tier or trial

The third of the sales trio ensures that a developer gets a chance to try your product without paying anything. Of course, everyone likes free stuff, so a developer would love to have some level of unpaid usage forever. And they'd prefer not to even get out their credit card. But a trial with a supplied card works fine.

It's not always feasible to provide free service indefinitely and developers shouldn't expect it. Since a free trial is fairly standard, this element is weighted at a high level in the DX Index.

6. An obvious place for questions

For both the initial experience and ongoing needs, developers may look for support. Often, there's not a way to get in touch and certainly not one that is developer-specific. Make sure your contact page feels reliable (is that a black hole, or do they actually respond?) and include pictures of your team, if possible. Give developers the feeling that, when they do have a question, it will receive an answer.

Since asking questions is how developers learn, this element is weighted at a high level in the DX Index.

7. API status information

Developers expect reliability from the APIs they consume. After all, when they integrate with your API, it becomes part of their stack. When problems arise in their own applications, developers want to understand which dependencies could be the issue. A transparent page with as much information as possible is key to supporting your developers.

API status gets a high weighting in the DX Index, as well, because it's an important element of trust—if something is wrong, a developer wants to know the truth.

8. Accurate API reference

Ask a developer about API frustrations and inaccurate document-ation tops the list. As with status, a developer must trust your product. One of the major violations of trust is an inaccurate, incomplete, or outdated API reference. As your API evolves, so must all of your documentation, especially the reference, which operates as your source of truth.

Since your API reference touches every stage of the developer experience, it is weighted at a high level in the DX Index.

9. Sample applications for download

Developers likely come to your product with a specific use case in mind. When you have an example that is close to their use case, they will move more quickly toward a prototype or even production application. The samples you make available—and their supporting tutorials and other documentation—enable developers to work much faster.

31

Since sample applications help developers reach their first success, it is weighted at a high level in the DX Index.

10. Recent developer blog posts

In giving a developer product the sniff test, a blog shows where a company is focused. If the most recent post was six months or a year ago, that looks pretty bad. If your last several posts are promotional or not very technical, that's a strike against you. After all, how do they know you understand their problems if you haven't articulated them?

While blog posts are an important tool for developer marketers, they aren't among the first things a developer cares about. This element has a medium weighting in the DX Index.

11. Interactive documentation

It used to be that an API explorer or other tool to see your product in action was rare. Now it's fairly simple to generate documentation that allows live, inline calls. You can take it further to build dashboards or sandboxes that allow similar interaction, which enhances the developer experience. If they can try something, they can better understand it.

Since interactive documentation isn't necessary for a good developer experience, it has a medium weighting in the DX Index.

12. Prominently-featured documentation

If someone arrives on your company home page, can they win a game of "find the API?" In other words, do you prominently link to your portal or documentation from within your site navigation?

If not on top, is it in the footer? Do you dedicate a section (or the entirety!) of your company's primary landing page to the developer audience?

It's not possible for every company to place a "developers" link in their top navigation. While incredibly important for API companies (where the direct customer is developers), this element has a medium weighting in the DX Index.

13. Example cURL calls

Much of a developer's work-life happens in the terminal command line. Often that's where they can work faster, without pointing and clicking. When you provide example cURL calls, you make it easier for them to move from conceptual (your documentation) to actual results they can see. In addition to cURL examples, you could include copy-paste API key or other tokens. For some, a dedicated command line interface (CLI) is another way to improve the experience on a developer's local machine.

Example cURL calls are one of those features that developers love when present, but might not miss otherwise. That fact makes them nearly optional and a medium weighting in the DX Index.

Don't Wait for Perfection

It's important to create a foundation to help developers be successful with your product. Fix the biggest gaps first, then make a plan to address others in the future. Even the best developer companies cannot provide a perfect developer experience.

Once you have a handle on where you're sending developers, you're ready to reach more of them. Content is one of the best ways to find developers when they're ready to learn. The next several chapters address different types of content that will attract your technical audience.

BLOG POSTS

Reach More Developers with Frequent, Helpful Articles

Every year thousands of amateur players register for the Major League Baseball (MLB) draft. Many of these men (and they're all men, for now) will never play a game for one of the 30 major league teams. In fact, only 900 will be drafted and agree to a contract with a professional organization, which include multiple levels of minor leagues. A young man in the United States has a greater chance of being poisoned than being paid to play baseball.

Of those that make it to the biggest stage, the very best play 20 years. On average, an MLB player has about five years of service before retiring. With a roster size of 750 across all teams, that's a lot of turnover. The reason for the MLB draft—and others like it across professional sports—is that there must always be a new group of up-and-coming players.

You want the same flow of developers being introduced to your company and product (though, hopefully you'll have a more diverse representation). But there's no such thing as a developer draft, where companies take turns laying claim to coders. Instead, everyone has access to the pool of potential developers who can even choose to work with multiple companies. Those sharing the best ideas will attract the most eyes. The best way I know of reaching developers is through frequent, helpful blog posts.

It's likely you already are publishing to a blog. That's good. A steady drum-beat of content is good for SEO and also makes it easier for you to continue. Consistency breeds consistency. However, as you attempt to meet your post quantity goals, you might be sacrificing quality. Your pieces may be too shallow or off-topic for your company. And, potentially, they aren't hitting the subjects that the right developers want to read.

Figure Out Who You Want to Reach

Even if your website messaging and portal experience are developer friendly, it's easy to let the blog slip into volume over value. Or, because it's difficult to find writers, you're willing to accept any topic. I've been there myself, which is how I became such a believer in publishing what interests a specific audience.

You probably already know many things about the developers you want to reach, but haven't yet articulated it. The more you know about them, the better your content can address their problems. And that's the key which unlocks successful blog content. There are topics that your developers will research, and you want them to find you during the process. If they bump into your blog headlines, you want them to feel it hit a nerve, so they'll click through to learn more.

It's rather difficult to do this without understanding a bit about the developers you want to reach, even at a high level. Ask yourself some of these questions:

- Do they work for big companies or startups?

- What programming language do they primarily use?
- Are they early in their career or just starting out?
- What's their team structure like and what's their role?
- What are some of the common titles they have?
- What departments do they support with their code?

You might not have all the answers, but it only takes a little bit of information for a picture to come into focus. Then you can combine that developer profile with your product. For example, if your product is an authentication API, how might a senior Python engineer at a startup use it? Perhaps a "move fast and break things" culture has them concerned security may be overlooked. Assuming you can gain their trust, your product would be an option that helps them build their own product more quickly, while remaining confident about security risks.

Leveraging even a small amount of information about your developer audience helps point you in the right direction. Based on these discoveries, you can more confidently arrive at educational topics that will help developers. In order to endear trust, you'll want to cover the areas of your product a developer would otherwise need to build on their own. For the authentication API example, you'd want to cover OAuth and other standards, authentication best practices, and modeling potential threats. You could also look at language-specific angles at authentication topics—Python frameworks and libraries, code snippets and sample apps specifically geared toward Python.

Keyword research can help you further hone both your high level and granular topic selection. Once you better understand the developer, you can determine the words they use to articulate their technical problems. Even better, SEO tools can tell you how popular some of those phrases are. Often, that unlocks additional topic ideas surrounding the problems.

Once you've determined who you want to reach with what content, you need to make it original. Every company has opinions—the organization was built upon them. There's a reason your product was needed, and its important differentiators are within that viewpoint. While your blog posts should always be outwardly-focused on the developer problems, each should harness the company point of view. What do you believe that competitors don't? Make sure your blog posts spread that belief.

Sometimes you won't know exactly who you want to reach and the problems they have, but the company opinions should be clear. Any of the three can change, or perhaps you'll find out your assumptions were wrong. Your blog posts can actually help you do that, gathering data on what is resonating and with whom. Expect to make some shifts in your understanding along the way.

With each blog post you pursue, you can return to these three areas and ask the questions:

- Who am I reaching?
- How can I share knowledge with them?
- What is the company viewpoint that will make this message most successful?

♯

On a macro level, you can use your understanding of audience, problems, and viewpoint to build a blog content calendar. This publication plan will map your broad concepts to specific topics and dates.

Make a Publication Plan

I grew up in the country on property next to an old two lane road. For entertainment, our dog would sit at the end of our driveway next to the road. Whenever a car would come by, she would bark and chase it all the way to the other edge of our property. It was a funny ritual and for all her effort, she naturally never caught a car. Of course, if she had caught the car, I'm not sure what she'd have done with it. A lot of activity does not mean you have a plan—and the plan is what makes the activity successful.

You may have big goals for your developer blog posts, or you might not have any concept of what you should create—but you know consistent publication is important. In either case, you need a plan to help you scope out your approach.

Start with where you'll publish your technical posts. Ideally, these are on your company blog aimed at a developer audience. If you're serious about reaching developers directly, you should already have a property with this type of content. If you don't, you probably shouldn't start one immediately. Taking on a new publication is a big undertaking. Too often, changing priorities or lack of momentum lead to inconsistency. Instead, start with posts to your existing blog until you have a cadence that warrants its own publication.

In some cases, you may be starting a new blog. The process of creating a developer content plan is the same, regardless of where the posts end up. For best success, you should:

1. Determine a cadence
2. Constrain your focus
3. Create a calendar
4. Choose initial topics
5. Share your calendar

6. Stick to the calendar

When I give talks on developer content, I'm often asked how many posts should be published. Often, that question comes with a timeframe: how many per month or how many per week. I half-jokingly say the answer is always the same: two. The timeframe determines the volume, because the person asking knows what's possible in their situation.

There is no right answer on volume. A fewer number of great articles will perform better than many low quality posts. However, consistent publication keeps you in the habit and gives you more chances to see what works with your developer audience. So, aim for a number that you can hit with quality content and adjust as you go.

Many EveryDeveloper clients publish weekly, which puts them between two per week and two per month. They've arrived there after considerable investment (internally and externally), consistency, and a lot of help. One mistake I've seen companies make is to choose a big number, then publish anything they can get written, regardless of topic. That's why a focus and a calendar are important parts of your publication plan. With an understanding of the developer problems you solve, you can better scope out some areas to cover.

In addition, I find it helpful to declare types of posts, so you have another way to constrain your topic selection. Here are some post types to consider:

- Tutorial: Walk through a specific problem and solution
- Vision: Share your technical thought leadership
- Best practices: Educate developers with practical tips
- Interview: Ask relevant questions of a developer influencer

- Comparison: Explain the pros and cons of two or more choices
- How we work: A technical look inside your organization
- Roundup: List of related technical choices with your analysis

You may come up with some types of your own. The key is to limit yourself to two or three types, then use those to plot out your calendar. For example, you might choose two tutorials, one best practice, and one roundup per month. You can put that on your developer content calendar as a placeholder for the next three months. Simply drop them in every Wednesday (or whichever day of the week you choose).

Fig. 6 Your Technical Content Calendar Can Start as a Simple Spreadsheet

That's the easy part. Now you need to get actual ideas for those posts. I've found this is much easier with a post type to work from. Connect your developer problems to specific post types and you'll more easily come up with ideas that fit your audience and product.

The idea stage can be a good time to bring in additional writers, either inside your organization or externally. When you provide some editorial constraints, you'll get better concepts from other writers, as well. "I'm looking for best practices on Python authentication" is much better than "want to write a blog post?"

For this reason, make sure your calendar and publication plan are visible to your entire organization. This will help share the work you're doing and make it clear what's coming next. It also enables you to get better contributions, because you've made clear how others can help.

To consider a topic complete on your calendar, it needs a few fields complete:

- Post type
- Author
- Draft headline
- Due date
- Publication date

You'll be tempted to write "Adam's Python post" or similar in the draft headline spot. Instead, try to come up with a good headline that you'd want to see on your blog—the sort of thing that would make your developer readers click. You want to make sure your efforts at understanding the problem and harnessing the company viewpoint come through. The headline can help keep you focused on a topic that will hit the mark, with your goals and your readers.

Finally, you'll want a due date and a separate (obviously later) publication date. This allows time for review and publication. And yes, the due dates sometimes slip. Planting a stake gives you a timeline to shoot for. As you scale your publication, you can build a backlog of drafts that can protect you from slipping deadlines.

Scale Your Publication

When you consistently publish new content on similar themes, you've taken the first steps toward treating your blog like an actual publication. You don't need to truly be an independent publication, publishing under a separate name on its own domain. To scale your efforts, it helps to think as if that was the case. What personnel would be needed for a newspaper or magazine? This thinking can help you expand your reach.

The content side of every publication has editors, contributors, and a process through which they collaborate. You'll want to define these elements as early as possible. In fact, your publication plan is the start of your editorial process. And by defining a focus, you've at least given yourself the title of interim editor-in-chief. It's up to you and your other responsibilities whether that becomes a permanent title.

There are other editorial roles, which may also fall to you in the early days:

- Managing editor: Handles day-to-day operations and article topics
- Section editor: Seeks contributions of specific content types or subjects
- Copy editor: Reviews contributions for structure and typos
- Similarly, there are different types of contributors to consider:
- Staff writers: Employees who contribute to the publication as part of their job
- Freelance writers: Contractors who pitch topics and write them as-needed
- Columnists: Internal or external contributors who bring a specific point of view

You can connect these various roles together with a simple editorial process, which you started in the previous section. You'll want to assign pieces to contributors, review the articles as they come in, and publish new posts on a set schedule. It takes significant effort to identify, produce, edit, and publish technical content. Working with outside writers and editors is an effective way to scale your publication, especially if you don't have the internal head count.

Even if there's a single person running the show, it helps to define the points in your process, so you can grow it to include others. You'll also want to include promotion of your published content within your workflow. At a minimum, you'll promote to your existing channels, which likely include social, email, and on your website. You can also consider other communities that could be a good fit, such as Hacker News or specific subreddits. Before you promote your own content within a community, make sure that's allowed. The best way to know the rules is to be an active member of the community, which is certainly a bigger commitment than a quick posting.

Another promotional angle that has gained popularity is republication. It used to be that duplicate content hurt your SEO, so marketers avoided it at all costs. You should still be careful to have a canonical version of each post on a site you control. However, search engines are smarter about which is the original, and there are tools you can use to specifically point to the canonical version.

The options for republication are always changing, but some popular choices to consider are:

- Medium
- Dev.to

- DZone

Finally, you might scale your publication by going broader on developer topics. The best way to do this is through testing and validation of what resonates with the audience you want to reach. For example, your specific Python posts might get traction amongst beginning or intermediate Python programmers. You could expand your area of coverage to include more general Python topics.

An editorial shift like this exposes you to a larger potential audience. The downside is it's less likely that developers have a problem your product solves today. However, as we've seen in other areas of developer marketing, great results come when you focus on the long term. You want to reach more developers with authentic, helpful content that educates and inspires. When they have the problems your product solves, you'll be top of mind.

TUTORIALS

Teach developers exactly how to solve their problems

Like any classic science fiction flick, *Star Wars* does not disappoint in terms of taking an ordinary individual and revealing the hidden powers within that transform him from a nobody to the hero that saves the day. Luke has returned speedily to Tatooine to discover his greatest fear – his aunt and uncle have been incinerated and his home decimated by an Imperial army. Whether because he has nowhere else to go or for the purpose of avenging his family, Luke puts his trust in Obi Wan and begins his journey to become the hero the resistance needs, though he has no idea of the power that lies within him.

Like Luke preparing for the journey to heroism, you sit reading a book about developer marketing. You might even be thinking of putting it down. Surely you can't learn anything new about tutorials that you haven't already seen. "Hello there," I say. "I'm here to call you to adventure and to give you the information you'll need on your quest. I cannot promise it will be easy—you will face many trials. Just when things are at their lowest point, when hope appears to be lost, you'll realize you had within yourself everything you need to conquer developer tutorials. Perhaps, the friends you meet along the way will also help you out."

Every story has a structure. In fact, Joseph Campbell dubbed it the Hero's Journey and you can map many famous stories to it, including *Star Wars*.

Tutorials also have a structure. To ignore the structure would be like Luke starting as a fighter pilot or the movie fading to black before he blows up the Death Star. You'll leave developers unfulfilled, even if they can't explain why. But they'll be able to tell you, quite clearly, that your tutorial isn't useful.

Structure does not mean you're constrained to a boring car manual experience. Just as there are many stories that all fit the Hero's Journey, you'll find many creative ways to serve developers with the articles you write to guide them through your instructions.

No content you produce will educate and inspire developers more than with tutorials. By their nature, tutorials are a solution, which means they can always be framed around a problem. Every content type can be problem-focused, but won't always express the solution the same way (if at all). On the other hand, tutorials are special in that they walk developers through the exact steps needed to reach an expected conclusion.

Tutorials are a foundational content type for developer companies. They can be included in documentation, blog posts, and many other places. Tutorials can also come in many different formats, such as video or interactive. Even within the range of the written word, there are many ways to show a tutorial's steps.

Before you get creative with the rules, it's important to learn them. From the general, you can then extract the specific for your situation.

The Ideal Tutorial Structure

Some tutorials are long, some are short. Some are very detailed, and others tell you the steps in broad brushstrokes. This chapter itself is sort of a tutorial. You have tutorials in many areas of your site (and possibly on other websites, too). When you write "how to" articles for your blog, they may seem different from your documentation. You may introduce your company or product, at least tangentially. Documentation can assume more knowledge, but any tutorial content will still use the same basic structure.

Here is the tutorial structure in four elements:

1. Explain the context
2. Show the end result
3. Walk through the steps
4. Help them take the next step

When tutorials get things wrong, they most commonly start—and end—with the third element. If you find the first three words of your tutorials are "in this tutorial," then you might have skipped ahead. Remember that every tutorial is a solution to a problem. The context, which comes at the beginning of each tutorial, explains that problem. How will the reader know you'll solve their problem if you never mention the problem?

Imagine your friend handed you a folded piece of paper. You open it up and see this list:

- Branch
- String
- Hook

Strangely, before you even had a chance to look at the paper, your friend disappeared. You're left to wonder how big of a branch to get and what type of string. Do you need a Captain Hook hook, or will a jacket hook suffice? Even with detailed instructions for each item on the list, you could still be lost. Wouldn't it mean much more if your friend said they were going to teach you to go fishing? That's the power of context, and your tutorial needs it—even a little bit helps a lot.

You can get by without explicit context as long as there's some vision of where you're headed. An average tutorial begins with the end result, which should be the second element of a great tutorial. If there's a user interface to what you're building, you can show a screenshot near the beginning of the tutorial. Whether visual or written, you need to give readers an idea of where you're headed. Not many developers will blindly follow some steps without some explanation of the reward.

Now you're ready to begin the steps of the tutorial. For a written piece of content, you may only be a paragraph or two in at this point. But that front matter matters. Developers may have some concept of what they're in for, but you can give them a better idea before you dive in. Let them know the number of steps and maybe even what's included in those steps. Make sure each step connects logically to the next. Periodically explain what you've already accomplished and what's coming next. The steps of a tutorial should feel like a friend guiding you through their list of items. Don't be the friend who disappears.

When you complete the tutorial, you're missing out of you Forrest Gump the ending. Among the catchphrases for this 1994 movie character is, "that's all I have to say about that." It worked for him, but developers want to know more. They've gone through this entire tutorial with you. Hopefully they have something working. The natural question is: what's next.

Help developers take the next step, which could be hosting their project, connecting it to another tutorial, or reading a specific area of the documentation to gain even more context. Include a call to action in every tutorial to keep them on their journey.

Developer Tutorial Best Practices

As you expand your tutorials, you'll find the approach that works best for you within the standard structure. For example, you'll discover the length that works for your developers, as well as the depth of technical detail. You might even find you have tutorials that cover the same topic in different ways, which can avoid the problem of fitting too much into a single piece of content. There's no need to take everything in these best practices as gospel, but I've learned some rules of thumb and things to avoid after writing developer tutorials for over 20 years.

You'll be tempted to cover everything in a single tutorial. Instead, it's better to ruthlessly cut the scope and make each tutorial hyper-focused. There must be some prerequisite knowledge that you can expect of your reader. If it's a Python tutorial, you must assume they've written some Python before, unless it's a complete beginner's tutorial. In the case of beginner material, you aren't likely to get into usage of an API with Python. You need to choose a scope—the smallest possible to make a useful tutorial—and stick to it.

I'm not a fan of specific prerequisite sections, with a list of things developers must do or know before beginning your tutorial. That feels like homework. These are extremely common, so this one may be a personal preference. I think it can be more naturally handled during the contextual introduction. The reader can then make the choice whether to continue with your more advanced tutorial without being called out explicitly by the prerequisites.

I don't think tutorials should "punt" on the concepts core to a developer's understanding of the tutorial. This term comes from American football, where a team kicks the ball downfield to give their opponent a worse field position. When making this choice, the team also gives up their turn on offense. When you link to another concept, without much coverage in your own post, you are essentially telling the reader that you don't want to help them understand. You'll need to weigh this against your desire to scope to a narrow topic, but you can find a balance that provides some context to what a developer would learn in another tutorial.

You'll remember from the previous section that it's important to share the end result near the beginning of your tutorial. Similarly, you also should share the route at a high level. Define the number of steps you'll share, then tell them what they'll learn in each step. You don't need to provide a verbose overview, because they'll learn the details in each step. However, a simple numbered list can help frame the tutorial to come.

In fact:

- Bullet points
- And other lists
- Are useful throughout

People skim online content, and developers may be even more likely to use this reading technique. When you break up your post visually with short bullet points, the reader's eye stops to see if it's important. Anytime you find yourself writing three or more items in prose form, see whether it looks better as bullet points. It almost always does.

Similarly, sub-headings can help keep the reader focused on the next task. They also catch the eyes of skimmers, perhaps more than bullet points. You can use these sub-headings as steps in your tutorial and even activities within each step. For the best results, write action-oriented sub-headings that are three to eight words long. Start with a verb to inspire motion and include enough detail to encourage more investigation.

While sub-headings split your tutorial into more granular sections, you can also use multiple pages for a similar effect. Developers can fully complete one page before clicking through to the next. A multipage approach also helps you see how far the average reader gets through the topic, which can help you identify trouble spots where you can provide better instructions.

If possible, provide a full page option for developers. Many technical readers like to "ctrl-f" a page to search for certain words. It can be frustrating to visit multiple pages in order to find out whether the concept is even covered. The one page approach can also be useful for printing—that's right, some people learn better when they can touch the paper.

In fact, using multiple formats can be a great way to cover topics in different ways. While most of what I've covered in this best practices section was focused on text, you can apply the tutorial structure (and many of these guidelines) to video and other content mediums.

Consider Alternative Formats

Despite the constraints mentioned in this chapter, there's a lot of room for creativity in your tutorials. This is especially true with the many formats you could use to educate your developers. Even within written content, there are many vehicles you can use to deliver a tutorial. However, chances are when you think alternative formats, there's one that immediately comes to mind: video.

Using your same structure, starting with context and the end result, you can record multimedia tutorials that show how to solve a developer problem. For these videos, you'll likely call upon a few different types of recording:

- Instructor on camera
- Audio of instructor
- Presentation slides
- Screencast of results
- Screencast of code

Each of these has a high quality bar on the modern web. Just as long-form writing is an important skill, it takes practice to create and edit great tutorial videos. At a minimum, you'll likely want to go up a level from your existing webcam and get a professional microphone. Add to that screencast software and the time it takes to learn it, and you have yourself enough work for multiple team members. Like written content production, this is one for a developer marketer to consider outsourcing.

Whether or not you do the video production yourself, you'll want to be involved in how you approach your tutorials. Done poorly, these videos can be too long, bland, and difficult to see. One successful way to combat all three is to aim for short, bite-sized lessons. Programming education company egghead.io recommends their instructors keep lessons to under 10 minutes. Many of their videos are less than five minutes.

Showing a lot of text via video is not the strong suit of the format. Nor is it the best way for a developer to copy code. That said, including code in your tutorial video is almost certainly a requirement. You can alleviate the downsides with a couple small adjustments:

- Make the full code available via download

- Increase the text size so it is most readable

Video loses quality and sharpness when streamed—and developers won't always use full screen mode on their largest monitor. Plan accordingly.

∄

Short videos can work well alongside the multi-page tutorial approach. You'll need to spend a little more effort shaping each lesson if you want them to stand on their own. It's perfectly reasonable that a developer could land on step three, for example, without ever seeing the previous steps.

Like with other multi-page tutorials, you can easily use analytics to determine each step's success and where developers get stuck. You can also bring in a concept from online courses to mark particular steps "done," either automatically or when a developer specifically clicks a button. With a little engineering effort to persist this information, you'll also be able to see the average progress of developers—and even pinpoint which developers should get special attention (either for help through a rough patch or to recognize their efforts).

Playing videos and clicking through multi-page tutorials provide pretty basic interactivity. Some innovative tutorials go much farther. For example, you can bring the code editor experience into the web browser. Twilio, Stripe, and others have experimented with tutorial formats that blend instruction, code, and even outcomes. Imagine that your tutorials would highlight sections of code as each is described in a tutorial. Or explore the code and jump to the place where each line is introduced in the tutorial.

On the effort scale, these sorts of interactive experiences are much harder to pull off. You need a team with skills not just in technical writing and education, but also engineering. Based on how important particular topics are to your company, it could be worth the effort. For example, an interactive tutorial could get developers started faster and help them feel more connected to your product. For an API company, this type of tutorial is worth an exploration.

Fig. 7 Gaming Meets Developer Education in TwilioQuest

Famously, Twilio took interactive learning even farther than the browser. The latest version of its TwilioQuest game is a downloadable package. It features 8-bit-inspired graphics, an original soundtrack, and an expanding list of programming "missions." The company has seen success with onboarding developers and has also used the game for live trainings worldwide.

But you don't need to spin up an entire gaming division to create great tutorials. You can get creative with the mediums you have available. JavaScript innovator Dan Abramov used a simple email newsletter to teach developers important concepts of the language. GitHub created Learning Labs atop its existing code repository features of issues, pull requests, and comments.

Perhaps you could embed a tutorial within a sample app, which would allow developers to learn while exploring a working app. Or embed a code playground tool like Codepen and write your tutorial within code comments. The most important aspect of a tutorial is that it helps developers learn and have success with your product. The format is merely the vehicle that inspires them to complete it and internalize its lessons.

Tutorials can do their work at every stage of your marketing funnel and are even useful for existing customers. If your effort is to educate and inspire developers—and I think it should be—you will make liberal use of tutorials in all their forms. Simply follow the structure, be a guide to your developer hero, and may the force be with you.

GUIDES

Show How Deeply You Understand
What A Developer Needs

Just under eight inches long and sharpened to a long point, the Blackwing 602 might be the most heralded pencil in the world. Painted a deep black, the metal cap is clamped flat to hold its thin, pink eraser. A favorite of animators, it was discontinued in 1998, raising the price of a single pencil to $40 before another company began reproducing them. You can still find originals on eBay and creators buy them up to tap into that special something.

Disney animator Shamus Culhane, who led the original Snow White team and other famous movies, was buried with a Blackwing 602 in his hand. If he were still around, surely he could show you a thing or two about using this pencil. Like any tool, there are tricks to get the most out of it and intricate details to understand—like how to extend or replace the flat eraser with the built-in clip. However, using this iconic pencil will not make you an animator. That requires a whole other level of instruction.

Similarly, developer guides go well beyond the tools that are used. An individual tutorial may be rooted in a problem, but its details are in the technical solution. A guide takes a much broader view, with less emphasis on tools. It unpacks the details within the problem and best practices that set the context for a solution. Since there's much more involved in a guide, they are typically longer. While you may produce dozens of tutorials, you'll typically need fewer guides.

The Developer Content Mind Trick

A landspeeder approaches a checkpoint, waved to a stop by a group of stormtroopers. You're likely familiar with the line that comes next: "These aren't the Droids you're looking for."

The Jedi mind trick—using the Force to implant a suggestion in the minds of those they encounter—is useful in a galaxy far, far away, but is also a valuable approach for your guide content. As in all developer marketing, you want to teach more than promote. With your guides, this is especially true. To promote your product, you don't promote it.

In fact, the best guides actively tell developers how not to use a product. Developers like to solve problems, so they naturally gravitate toward building a solution themselves. Even as they skeptically review your product, they'll be estimating what it will take to recreate. The reality is developers are usually underestimating the effort required. Before they understand a problem, they haven't found all the edge cases and time-consuming rabbit holes.

Your guides can tap into a developer's desire to build it themselves. At the same time, it can walk them through all the things they're missing in their estimation. Give them a blueprint and you'd think they'd go build it. Many will instead realize how hard it is—and how much better it would be to use your product. That's the mind trick.

Gremlin provides developers tools for engineering resiliency and backs them up with in-depth guides. The concept behind its products is called "chaos engineering," which imagines a monkey shutting off servers randomly. A system that can withstand that sort of chaos has built-in resilience. Gremlin's largest traffic driver is its *Chaos Monkey Guide for Engineers*, a nearly 20,000 word unpacking of best practices and background. If you're serious about improving your engineering operations, landing on that guide should build trust that Gremlin can help.

Fig. 8 Gremlin's Guide Is Rich with Knowledge, Nearly 20,000 Words, and Available to All

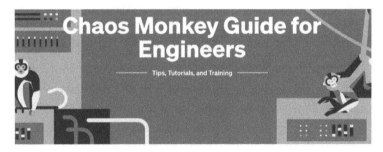

In 2010 Netflix announced the existence and success of their custom resiliency tool called *Chaos Monkey*.

What is Chaos Monkey?

In 2010, Netflix decided to move their systems to the cloud. In this new environment, hosts could be terminated and replaced at any time, which meant their services needed to prepare for this constraint. By pseudo-randomly rebooting their own hosts, they could suss out any weaknesses and validate that their automated remediation worked correctly. This also helped find "stateful" services, which relied on host

The keywords used to describe the problem should gather search traffic and introduce developers to your company. SEO is likely to be a major source of guide traffic. You should research and declare those important company keywords before writing a guide. Either high volume or low competition will make keywords more likely to be worth the effort. Most likely, you'll find a combination of medium volume and medium competition for your desired terms. If there's a chance you could rank on the first page of results, it's worth going for these words that fit your company. Don't get too hung up on a single page of results—there should be many variants that can combine to bring the right developers to your guide.

Done right, guides are helpful at every stage in the funnel. Even if a developer discovered you elsewhere, the guide would reinforce their desire to solve the problem. You can include your guide, or at least the lessons it covers, in your onboarding emails. Use one of the guide's core concepts as the foundation for a webinar offered to developers who signed up and are still evaluating your product.

Finally, for those deep in the funnel, you can point them to the guide (perhaps for a second or third time). You will be demonstrating your expansive understanding of the topic, solidifying your authority. Why would a developer build it themselves or choose a competitor when they can buy from the ones who best solve it? That's you, as demonstrated by your guide.

Every developer company should have at least one topic where they have this kind of authority. I call the deepest of these guides "Signature Content," because it's what separates you from others. Someone can copy your product, but it's much harder to copy how deeply you understand and communicate a problem.

Gated Content Versus Open Content

Guides traditionally live their life over in the "resources" section of a product's website. Here they get a short landing page to describe their content. Anyone who makes it through the gauntlet of your form (usually name and email address, sometimes several fields more) gets to download the PDF for later reading. This "gating" of the guide has some serious downsides, especially for developers.

For one, developers are notoriously skeptical of marketing. Exchanging an email address to read what you have to say (with no guarantee that it will even be the technical information they seek) is straight out of a marketer's playbook. Many developers will close their web browser instead of add themselves to your funnel. Those that do give you an address may make it disposable—and certainly not the "work email" you ask them to include.

Many marketers gladly trade this skepticism for an email address. It fits their metrics and there are some real leads that come through using gated content. However, when you go this route, there are upsides to open, non-gated content that you leave behind.

The search engine traffic that deep guides provide will always outrank the lighter resource landing pages. There's just a lot more keywords to rank and links are typically concentrated on the guide's primary page. You're unlikely to get links to a simple page that clearly leads to a marketing funnel. And links are an important factor in search engine rankings, especially for competitive terms.

Similarly, developers will share a truly helpful guide that is open for anyone to read. You'll see tweets and forum posts around the best developer content. When your guide is open, developers will also share internally. A mention in an internal email or Slack message could be the referral that encourages someone to take a look at your product. This word of mouth is much less likely with a limited landing page.

You can still use gated content alongside your open content. With this approach there are two likely choices:

1. The exact content, in PDF form
2. Complementary content

It may seem strange to gate content that is already available publicly. However, by their nature guides are long. Many thousands of words are required to reach the depth needed for your topic. You've also likely separated the guide into multiple pages. The web may not be the best format for someone to read. So, you can provide an option—in exchange for an email address—to download a PDF of your guide. As with other resources, you'll want to create a pleasing design and invest in proper layout. Now you have the upsides of non-gated content traffic and still have a method to get email addresses from the most serious of leads.

Fig. 9 Example of a Gated Resource Which Requires Developers Share Personal Information

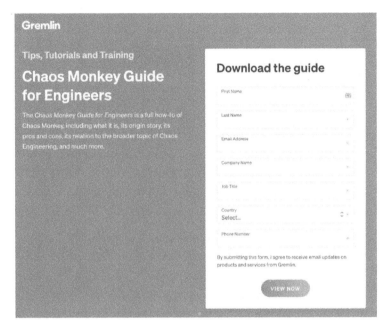

Simultaneously, you've created more trust with developers who won't see the gate as a ploy. If you've already shared the content, surely the PDF option is just for their benefit. Now those who want to read all of your guide or aim to share with teammates will download it. You may have fewer email addresses overall, but they'll be much more valuable.

Instead of the full PDF download, you might offer something else that is related to the guide. For example, an email course or files that help them get started might be something a developer would consider. If there's a natural case to make for why you'd need their email address to deliver these, that's all the better.

Even if it is simply a way to get them in your system, you'll have built trust by providing a really valuable guide on the open web for all to read.

Take Your Message to Other Channels

A deep, helpful guide is only the beginning. It provides the foundation for many other campaigns and content pieces you can create. You can use them to get more value out of the guide, add more value into the guide, or both. In the previous section we saw how you could use both gated PDF and open content versions of the same guide. Similarly, you can bundle and unbundle it in many other ways.

The most natural approach is to take pieces of your guide and turn them into blog posts. The simplest way is to use the actual content of the guide, but a more valuable approach is to take a new angle on existing material. You might write a series of blog posts on one concept within the guide, expanded to different industries. Or create tutorials using multiple languages and frameworks to bring the guide's concepts into reality. Each blog post or other piece of content can link back to the guide as reference. This helps more developers discover the guide, as well as signal the importance of the guide to search engines.

Your unbundled content doesn't even have to live on your own site. You can write guest posts for relevant developer sites or on partner blogs. Either write them new for a publication or use the republication concepts from the blog post chapter. Each piece of content should be valuable on its own, but also point back to the primary guide.

Your guide could also perform double-duty via video. There are many topics within the broader guide that could be turned into slides and recorded. Or have an engineer describe the more technical aspects of the guide with a whiteboard. You could even let developers sign up for a multi-hour video course version of your guide.

Other channels and mediums to consider:

- Daily email course
- Short explainers on YouTube
- Monthly webinars on different concepts
- Conference talks by engineers
- Half-day workshops
- Distribute on course platforms
- Break the guide into LinkedIn posts

That list could go on—and you should brainstorm on your own with knowledge of your own product and available channels.

Most important as you consider the guides you might produce is to choose important topics for your product and the developers who might use it. Then frame your guide around the problems within that topic and explain solutions outside of your own product. Certainly, it's worth mentioning the company and even examples of success, but great guides should stand on their own. You want developers to learn and get help from the guide without needing to become a customer to capitalize on its lessons.

By taking this approach, where you intentionally focus away from your product, it creates a strange gravity that will pull developers toward you. They'll see your authority on the topic, and your product—which complements the viewpoint of your guide—will seem like the inevitable next step. In time, like the Blackwing 602, you'll become the obvious tool used by every developer who encounters the problems your guide so deftly explains.

EVENTS

Meet Developers Where They Are with Authentic Interactions

A tourist wanders along 57th Avenue in New York City, lost. The bustle of the city rushes past him, forcing him into the "slow lane" of the sidewalk. When a cab pulls up to the curb, he spots his chance. Wading through the river of people, he approaches a woman with a violin case getting out of the car. "How do you get to Carnegie Hall," he asks.

You probably already know the punch line: "Practice."

Now imagine that tourist was instead an aspiring musician, and the question really was about appearing on that impressive stage. The answer would be equally unsatisfying and not nearly as funny. That's how I felt when a young marketer once asked me how they could get clients like one of the well-known companies working with EveryDeveloper. My honest—and completely unhelpful—response was: "Meet the contact ten years ago when they were at a different company."

As much as I believe in content to reach developers and connect with their problems, there is something special about events. Many companies use them to generate leads, which may be successful in certain industries. For developers, new business should rarely be the primary motivation. Instead, use the lens of "educate and inspire" to introduce your product to a technical audience in an authentic way.

There are many ways to be involved in these developer events and a few different types. There are traditional conferences, where you can sponsor, speak, or simply attend. There are also more technical deep-dive events, such as hands-on workshops or ideative hackathons. Finally, you might explore virtual versions of these events or consider hosting webinars of your own.

The setting and expectations may be different, but you can use the same approach to successfully reach developers.

Fig. 10 Engineer Jessica West Finishes A Talk at DevRelCon London

Get the Most Out of Any Developer Conference

I have stood in a small booth within the giant expo hall, smiling at people passing by. In the earliest hours of the morning, I entered as a developer evangelist. By 9:30, I was feeling like a carnival barker. "Step right up, get your cloud-based software!"

Granted, even in my life as a developer, I always considered myself a technical communicator. In a professional sense, that made me an accidental marketer. Standing in that huge convention center room, surrounded by hundreds of other vendors, felt like the biggest accident of all. Yet, I had good conversations that day. I met people we could really help. I collected a pocketful of business cards, a few of which even had promise. And, from a personal perspective, the guy at the booth next door became that client 10 years later.

In a world where everyone acknowledges serendipity's role, large conferences introduce the setting where it can take place. "Planned serendipity" seems like an oxymoron, but I don't know how else you can explain the purpose of those large expo halls. For connecting with developers, serendipity has to be part of the plan. However, there are a few ways to have it play in your favor.

When sponsoring a developer conference:

- Have a plan to stand out
- Be involved in multiple ways
- Focus on the developer

彑

I've never worked for a company with a sports-style mascot. But I hope whoever puts on that mask before trotting out through the conference knows they are the most valuable player in the game that day. You don't need to create a gimmick to be noticed by developers, but you do need to think about what will draw attention. The alternative—quietly standing around and waiting to be noticed—is clearly a waste of money.

Some of the best approaches I've seen from conference sponsors have included puzzles or similar contests of skill. Developers love to tinker with problems and figure out how things work. If you can inspire them to grapple, you're more likely to make a lasting impact. Sure, entice them with a prize, but it's secondary to the experience.

Similarly, you can create an interactive exhibit. It could be physical, or even on a computer. Don't make it simply a demo of your product—go beyond that to capture the imagination of developers passing by. You could even make it something they can access from their phone, so then the most introverted of developers can take part. As with any developer content, you want to make sure it resonates with them. If you don't have the technical background of your audience, find someone who can help you tap into the authentic voice.

One way to amplify your sponsorship is to find other ways to be involved. The best among these is a speaking slot. While some conferences will give you a stage to pitch, others only accept speakers chosen for their merits alone. In either case, your approach should be the same: in every message, provide helpful advice on developer problems.

Sometimes this can be a difficult angle to take when you have, say, 30 seconds in front of 500 developers. This moment is made for a pitch, but it's unlikely someone will pull out their phone and sign up immediately. But you can entice them to seek you out at the conference with a mention of your puzzle contest or other stand-out feature. Your pitch should be for the opportunity to connect with them further.

A full conference talk is an even better way to pull developers close. You should take the same approach with a presentation as you would with a blog post: focus on a problem, which can be explained in a way that weaves your product in *without* a blatant pitch. Conferences typically won't allow commercials from the stage, and developers won't listen if it gets too promotional. Instead, speak as a peer from an area of experience.

If you don't personally have the background to produce an authentic talk, look for a member of the team that does. In smaller companies, a technical founder is a good choice. A senior engineer who really understands the gotchas of your product's problem-set is also a solid choice. For the right conference and audience, a newer engineer (either to the company or workforce) could help bring the empathy of "beginner's mind." Finally, developer evangelists/advocates and technical product managers should be able to give a great developer talk, as well.

In addition to speaking, do your best to attend the conference. If you've sponsored, you likely have a handful of tickets. Provide some of those to engineers who can help out with authentic conversations and expand the serendipity surface area. Speaking, attending, and sponsoring a conference can help with recruiting efforts, as well.

Finally, look for other opportunities to be involved. If there's a speaker dinner and you're invited, attend it. Great conversations happen over these meals. Similarly, you can arrange something similar with your partners or customers you know are attending. Look for ways to help out the organizers, whether it's with constructive feedback or an extra hand to carry something. Many will be on the lookout for ways to return the favor. Plus, if it's a small event, they need all the help they can get—and you can be an important partner now and in the future.

Participate in Hackathons for the Right Reasons

"Let's work for free, using other people's products, stay up all night, and see what we build." It's a concept so crazy, it just might work. In fact, it has worked, as thousands of developers come together to participate in hackathons every weekend.

There are a number of ways to structure hackathons, and the stereotype of late night pizza noshing isn't always part of its makeup. The general idea is for developers to team up to try out a new idea in a constrained timeframe—from part of a workday to two or three days maximum. Often these events are open to the public and they tend to skew younger. In fact, many of the hackathons that happen in person are for college or high school students.

You might also see online hackathons and contests, which aim at a broader demographic. Due to the time-shifting that's possible here, many of these run for longer periods of time.

For the companies participating, there are two primary reasons why a hackathon would make sense:

Recruiting: Developers who write code on their own time are great hires.

Feedback: Hackathon developers will try something new and tell you what they think.

Neither of these reasons is a typical marketing metric, so it's unlikely they'll get you directly to your goals. However, if broad awareness with engineers early in their career is part of your strategy (and for some developer companies, this could make a lot of sense), hackathons could be useful. You also may be able to use stories about what the developers build to inspire use cases with your customers. Depending on the level of investment, developer marketers could see some halo effect from hackathons. It could be worth joining with another department that would see the primary benefit.

At some conferences and hackathons, you could have the opportunity to present workshops. The audience will determine whether these educational events can track to sales, but there could be other reasons to participate. In addition to recruiting and feedback, these are content gold mines. It might be difficult to get someone on your team to write a tutorial, but with a live workshop they've nearly done so. You could ask to record their screen or encourage one of the attendees to share notes in exchange for a blog post byline.

While hackathons and workshops may not directly move the metrics most marketers care about, look for ways to expand their impact. Interestingly, there might be more opportunity for re-use of workshop content if it happens virtually. In addition, these online events have an opportunity to reach more people and be more trackable.

Make an Impact with Your Virtual Events

As the pandemic raged in early 2020, most mid-year events were canceled or postponed. It was unwise to suggest anyone travel and engage with crowds of people. As the year continued, it became clear that organizers needed to adjust their plans. Instead of canceling, many switched to virtual events. After attending and speaking at several, it's clear the experience does not directly translate. The logistics and cost of virtual events are smaller, but everything else in organizing a great event is much, much harder.

For one, the competition in virtual events is greater than physical events. In addition to all the other online conferences, you must compete with existing webcasts, repositories of training content, and—perhaps the largest competitor of all—a vast sea of YouTube videos. Anything a developer wants to learn is easily searchable for the exact keywords to describe the problem they're curious about in that moment. When physical events work, it's because they break out of developers' typical context.

A great virtual event must take advantage of what makes it different from everything else on the Internet. Some categories to consider as you brainstorm your event's positioning:

- Access
- Interactivity
- Unique content

Technical experts are busy. Developers rarely have access to even the most giving open source contributors. Your virtual events—or those you sponsor and participate in—could give these tech superstars a stage. Like in live events, attendees can ask questions or provide a more exclusive option for roundtable discussions with the expert. Notice there hasn't been any mention of your product here. Keep the focus on what will bring the audience and they'll remember who made it possible.

Access to your team might attract interest, depending on the size of your company and the loyalty of your existing developer audience. To reach new developers, you likely need to start with problems and authentic discussion outside of your product's specific solution.

Connecting with other attendees—who are likely practitioners who care about similar things—is another draw of physical events. Use interactivity to bring these like-minded developers together. Here you'll compete with all the other things someone could be doing during a day, like grabbing lunch and answering email. Look for ways to give a taste of what they'd miss if they tuned out.

Look for ways to show the community that is present for your virtual event. Can people find each other before the event to make a plan for who they want to meet? Do you have ways for attendees to self-segment, such as by language, job role, or industry? Remember, with the savings of time and money from making your event virtual, you can afford to include some extra effort to differentiate your virtual event. If the numbers are small enough (say, below 200 or so), you may even be able to do some hand-curation for your attendees. It doesn't scale, but it also doesn't have to.

While the work needed to replace an annual physical event looms large, regular smaller events can be easier. The bar for these webinars is also high, but will have less expectations than a virtual event. Also, with a shorter timeframe (usually an hour versus a day or more), you can pack more potency. You want to avoid the temptation to go too cookie cutter. For these shorter events, you want to aim to be unique.

An outside expert guest is one approach to a great webinar. Developers are more likely to sign up to hear an unbiased opinion than what they think will be a sales demo. In fact, as with other successful top of funnel content, the least you make it about your company, the better. Don't expect your outside guest to be walking attendees through your product, for example. That's a waste of everybody's time. Instead, have them provide color commentary on the problem you solve or an industry-wide analysis that will be new to your developer attendees.

Remember that this is a long game, introducing developers to your company and product. Doing so through a name they already respect is a good start. Helping them with their problems in a way that grabs their attention will further endear them.

And if you enabled them to use their brain in a new way—even for a tech riddle they noodled within an expo hall—that provides a human connection that's really hard to replace. Sort of like a violinist giving directions to Carnegie Hall, there's only one truthful answer.

OPEN SOURCE AND COMMUNITY

Listen and Contribute to a Broader Group of Developers

The traveling salesperson problem is a set of quandaries in computer science that cannot be optimally solved. In them, you are given a list of cities and must create the best route for a salesperson to follow. What's rarely discussed is how the people in each city respond to the sales pitch of the peddler at their door. As we've seen, developers are skeptical, and the level depends on how actively you appear to be pushing for a sale.

Consider three different salesmen and how you'd feel if each showed up at your door around dinnertime:

1. The first notices dinner on the table and steps into your house. "You need these knives to cut your food. I'll sit down for dinner with you and show you how!"
2. The second is holding a casserole and offers to join your dinner. As you sit down, they immediately begin talking about knives.
3. The third notices you don't have a salad and offers to make one with the vegetables they've brought. As you

dine, they listen to you, thank you for the meal, and leave after any post-meal pleasantries.

Which one do you think is more likely to sell a specific knife when calling on you a week later? Obviously, all of them have a job to do, but the third approaches it like a long-lasting relationship. That's the approach that works with developers, especially within open source.

Open source is software with a license that allows anyone to use and modify it without paying any fee. Popular open source projects engage many developers to contribute code for the greater good. Often, they use the project in their day job, but it may also be a hobby, or simply something the developer does to give back. Because of this altruistic nature of open source, it's an especially touchy place for marketing.

How you approach open source will depend upon your company's existing relationship with it. If your developer product is dependent upon a specific open source project, you definitely need an open source marketing strategy. Even in the case of open source complementing your product, there's probably a way you should be involved with one or more projects. This chapter will look at how to approach those two scenarios, as well as a couple other methods that marketing can dabble—and even excel—with open source.

Your Product Depends on Open Source

Much of the Internet runs on open source software. From web servers like Apache to content management systems like WordPress, your product almost certainly uses open source. However, it may not depend upon it at a business or community level. When a product depends on open source, it means you're either providing a version of the software as a service or your product is directly within that open source ecosystem. In either of those cases, there's really not a choice about whether to include open source in your developer marketing. It's compulsory.

Supporting one or more open source projects is not only a marketing decision when the company or product depends upon it. You'll likely employ many members of the open source community within your engineering, product, and other departments. For most companies that provide a particular open source product as a service, founders are often the originators of the project, or at least committed contributors. Your success depends upon the open source project's success, though often there are marketing distinctions you'll need to make, such as what goes in the commercial versus open source version.

Even if your product isn't an open source project, you may find yourself dependent upon open source communities. For example, many popular open source projects create a plugin architecture to keep the code base simple. Rather than accepting every single feature from the community—or the need to determine what is accepted and what is not—they'll create a way to extend functionality. When your product is a plugin or similarly a feature within another ecosystem, you are entirely dependent upon that project's survival. Again, it makes sense to support the project at a level beyond marketing. However, as a developer marketer, the open source community may be your primary channel.

The methods you use to reach an open source community may look a lot like those already discussed in this book. You'll want to understand the problems that developers have and how your product solves them. The non-promotional approach with which you reach an open source community is further amplified. Open source developers expect you to support the project because it benefits the entire community. And if your company or product depends upon the project, that approach makes even more sense.

Fig. 11 Try Elastic Hosted Search Service or Download Open Source Elastic Search Tool

Open Source Complements Your Product

Even if your product does not depend on a single open source project, it may be aligned very closely with several. In this case, you may find support at your company level, or be alone in seeing the potential from a marketing perspective. Either way, it's likely you'll interact differently with these open source communities, because there isn't a single one that your company depends upon. However, multiple open source projects mean you can try different approaches, especially with content, to see what resonates.

Developer products are often multi-purpose solutions, which makes them both valuable and a potential challenge from a marketing perspective. When you're clear about your use cases, it becomes easier to see how your product can complement a user of an open source project.

For example, let's say your product ingests logs from various services and provides a single repository to search and filter these logs. There are many reasons why someone would want to consolidate logs. And once your product has consumed the data, there are many ways you might allow developer customers to analyze it. One use case might be a data dashboard, and you could offer connections to various visualization tools, many of which are open source. Or perhaps customers want to aggregate the raw data into summaries stored in their own databases. You could offer connections to popular open source databases, with periodic updates as the data changes.

Even with these two use cases, there are a handful of complementary open source projects. Within each, there are dozens of content opportunities, including blog posts, tutorials, and even authority-driving guides. While the problems you discuss in these pieces would not always be specific to a single open source project, developers might be searching with a particular tool in mind. You would aim to have the answer for that developer across several potential projects.

Find Communities to Try Your Product

The further you get from a specific implementation, the harder it is to make a case that a community can be a direct channel for developer acquisition. Nevertheless, you may be able to find broad open source projects where the developer users match your audience. In this case, the open source can likely be applied to many different problems, with most falling outside of your purview.

One type of open source project that attracts large communities of developers is programming language frameworks. For example, frontend JavaScript has dozens of potential tools, such as React and Vue, each with vibrant communities ready for you to join. You can certainly make sure that your product supports them with libraries and examples, but that's not the end of joining a community. Resources for your own product create an easy entry point for the community to you, but you still need to show you care about being in their community.

For many marketers, it may be overwhelming to join an open source community. Whoever interacts with the developer members of the community should be capable of an authentic technical conversation. Depending upon the open source project and marketer, you may be the best possible choice. In other cases, you'll want an engineer, developer advocate, or similar technical role to interact with an open source community. They'll be able to represent your company and product in the community, which will help you identify the problems to help the community solve.

When you spot opportunities to help the community, you want to give away your solution as a tool or content. Sometimes, there's a place to include your product. Other times, simply seeing your name alongside the solution to their problem is enough. The marketing goal for joining a community is for its members to think of you when they need what your product offers. Like much of developer marketing, this is a long term commitment, not a one-time conversion.

Some may wonder about building their own community. In general, it's easiest to look for communities to join and support first. When your product gains enough interest of its own, you can consider how to tap into a community which has grown organically. You can certainly take some steps to encourage the formation of a community by providing a place for discussion. In general, this is difficult to completely bootstrap, because it will begin as a very small group. The most natural place for such a community to start is through your own useful open source projects.

Release Open Source as Marketing

Your company may not depend on open source for success, but you can still create open source as a marketing initiative. In fact, for some projects focused on your product, it's nearly a requirement. In other circumstances, you can endear yourself to a community by making a tool that solves a developer problem available for anyone to use and improve.

Start with your existing product and the tools to support it. For example, your API likely includes client libraries, which developers either download or install via package managers. The source code within these SDKs should be open source. Work with your team to make it available in a public repository, such as on GitHub. Then you'll need to be on the lookout for issues and pull requests from developers who use these libraries. For developer companies, this sort of product-focused open source is a great place to start. SDKs greatly increase a developer's initial experience with an API and also make it easier for them to update their integration in the future.

Another area to consider for open sourcing is your documentation. Technical writing likely isn't the first thing you think of with open source—it's mostly copy, not code, after all. However, often there is some code or process required to spin up your documentation site, such as connecting a static site generator. Plus, developers are used to working in GitHub, and you can streamline their documentation feedback by allowing them to submit their own edits. Someone on your team will always be able to approve, reject, or change the edits anyone submits. To fully embrace your developer community, you can extend edits to your entire site— yes, even the marketing pages.

Along with your SDKs and documentation in public code repositories, you can extend it to other areas of developer experience. Sample apps and tutorials, for example, are an extension of documentation. You can include them here, as well. Do you have an OpenAPI, JSON Schema, or other description of an API or its data? Open source these, as well.

Developers admire (and, in some cases, expect) this sort of transparency. For anything that is public already, there's little downside to making it open source. The only requirement is that you listen for feedback, something you should already be doing as you interact with developers.

When you open source the elements of your own product, you gain respect of the developers who have already found you. However, these aren't ways to help new developers discover your product. As an awareness or acquisition channel, you'll likely need some code that isn't directly related to your product. The next chapter digs into Tools as Marketing. As you read about this strategy, consider whether it would make sense to open source the tool.

TOOLS AS MARKETING

Build Something the Right Developers Will Want to Use

As a child, I spent a lot of time at my grandmother's house, which had been in the country one generation earlier. Now, the creek that bordered her property shared a neighbor in the first grocery store to come to her little town. My cousins and I considered that shopping center part of her property and would run wildly around, inside and out. Inevitably, we'd end up at one certain corner of the store, not the place you'd imagine would be of interest to children: the pharmacy.

That's because this new grocery store's pharmacy had the most advanced technology anywhere in the town. There was a wooden desk, with a built-in chair and TV screen, sitting right outside the pharmacist's window. One by one, we kids would take turns sitting at that desk. After placing a tiny arm through a permanently-attached cuff, we'd press the green button on the tabletop to commence the arm tightening. This public blood pressure machine kept us entertained for what must have been many annoying minutes for the staff.

Of course, that machine was doing its job. It wasn't coin operated, this was a free resource for the community, though meant for adults concerned about their blood pressure. It's not like someone using this machine was expected to immediately buy hypertension medication (they'd need to see a doctor for a prescription). Instead, I think it was meant to get shoppers to associate this new store with their health—and, perhaps, their medications. That machine, which entertained me as a child, was a physical example of using tools as marketing.

Three Developer Startups That Hurled

When your entire company is an API, it's really important to easily test API requests. That's how Twilio ended up buying a little developer project called Hurl. The simple website, built at a hackathon in 48 hours, can make API requests and inspect them right in your browser. Now it's been part of the story of three developer startups, all dependent upon APIs. While each used the Hurl differently, they started with the knowledge that developers want an easy way to test out requests and responses with an API.

The team at Twilio was already the biggest user and referrer to Hurl before they acquired it. When developers would write into Twilio support, the reply would often require an example API call. There are many ways for someone to try out an API, but most of them require special tools. Twilio support wanted a friendly tool that wouldn't take their customer additional time to install or set up. Hurl could help them provide a useful reply that was quick to understand.

After evangelizing Hurl to hundreds of developers, the site had a following of its own, even outside Twilio usage. Since the original creators had moved on to other projects, Twilio purchased Hurl so the company could maintain this important support tool. In time, it also became a marketing tool, as developers learned of Twilio through Hurl.

However, it wasn't core to Twilio's communication API products. Keeping the code maintained and the servers running became a burden, one a former Twilio evangelist was happy to take on. A new company, Runscope, took over Hurl and used it to acquire more targeted customers. The company's API inspection tools were a great match for Hurl. Chances are, if you had a one-off API call to review, you might have ongoing needs around Apis. The hunch paid off, as Hurl and other developer tools became referrers, either directly or via retargeted marketing, for Runscope's trial and paid product.

Fig. 12 Runscope Community Tools Page, circa 2015

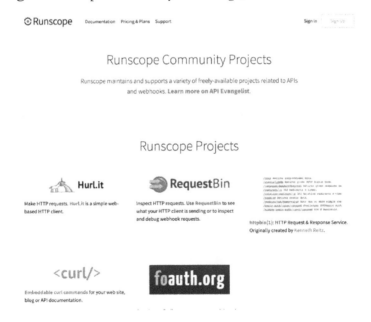

Eventually, the company moved toward more enterprise accounts and Hurl was less useful for potential leads. A third company, Insomnia, used the site to acquire customers of its API request client. Rather than siphon off leads, Insomnia redirected visitors to its installable software available only for Mac. The community tool aspect of Hurl went away and with it a lot of the usefulness for developer marketing. However, Insomnia became the third startup to gain traction off a single, simple developer project built in two days.

Now the Hurl domain is owned by a squatter, but the three startups went on to various levels of success. Insomnia was acquired by API platform Kong. Twilio is now a publicly-traded company and darling of Wall Street investors. And Runscope hit profitability before selling to software conglomerate CA Technologies, now a part of Broadcom. Though the story of Hurl has come to a close, the developer tool as marketing approach remains a popular way to gain mindshare, links, and traffic with developer audiences.

The Runscope Playbook

With Hurl's success, Runscope looked to expand its reach with more developer tools. It acquired and sponsored several others, testing the waters to see what would drive traffic and signups to their product. Each required a little up-front effort, either to build or negotiate, then the team could keep an eye on its results. When something didn't work, they'd close it down to focus resources on the tools which delivered the best. At its height, there were nearly a dozen developer tools on its community projects page.

The second-most popular tool for Runscope was Requestbin, which was a companion site to Hurl. Also acquired from Twilio, Requestbin showed API requests from the server perspective.

Rather than initiating calls from Requestbin, it receives requests, such as from a Webhook. These notifications, used by Twilio and other API companies, are often difficult to debug. With your own unique Requestbin URL, you could have a place to review the payload of each request without a bunch of setup.

Some of the other tools Runscope developed, acquired, or sponsored:

- Authentication testing
- Embeddable cURL commands
- JSON object generator
- API changelog service
- HTTP status code reference
- Mock API server

Each tool linked to Runscope and also embedded a tracking pixel for retargeted ads. The results were that Runscope was able to acquire the right developers for less than other methods. The company also used content, events, and other developer marketing techniques. But developer tools were the channel that performed the best.

Fig. 13 JAMstack Static Generator Tool Filtered for JavaScript

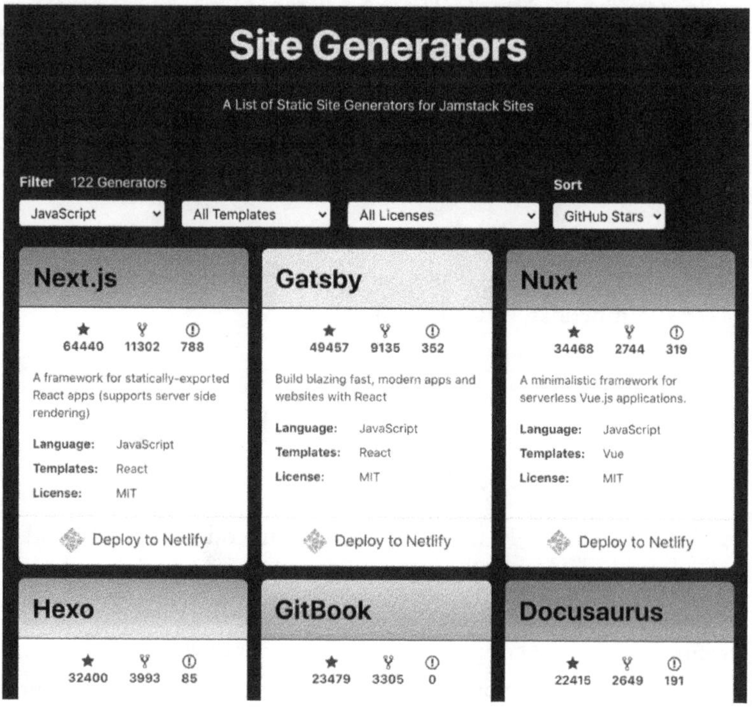

In a talk at Heavybit Accelerator, Runscope founder John Sheehan identified three rules for using the Runscope playbook:

1. Don't require a sign up
2. Do one thing well
3. Make it free

As you can see, these are similar to the approach you might use to create great developer content or a successful developer event. These developer tools focus on a problem, give away a useful solution, and let the provider's product ride its draft.

Developers are more likely to share a tool that doesn't have a catch—such as a required signup or a paid plan. Just like a gated guide, a simple tool that requires an email address will increase skepticism. Finally, it's easier to recommend something that solves a specific problem rather than a multipurpose tool.

For the same reasons these rules make a tool shareable, developers are also more likely to link to tools that check all three boxes. And links are an important part of what will make these tools rank in search engines. Without a lot of content, they need links to supply both the authority and the context (through the link text).

Netlify is one of several startups that have followed the Runscope approach, with a good amount of success. The company, which specializes in fast websites, often achieves its promise through static content. Early on, it created a comparison of static generator tools that developers use to make Netlify-ready sites. It now includes a database of over 300 tools, which can be filtered, browsed, and search by various features.

Once developers choose to build static websites, they often search for a way to organize their content. Headless CMS tools are a popular choice of static site developers, so Netlify added another resource to compare these tools. There are nearly 100 of these CMS products, compared on the factors a developer would consider when choosing one.

In fact, Netlify has now merged these two resources into a single page about JAMstack, the pattern of developers merging JavaScript, APIs, and Markdown.

With this single site, Netlify combined a guide approach with its two developer tools to build an ultimate resource, which now also includes a Slack community and conference.

Find Your Targeted Developer Tool

Now you are ready to follow in the footsteps of Runscope, Netlify, and others with a simple developer tool you can use as marketing. As with content, you'll want this tool to provide developers with the solution to a common problem. Unlike content, which might discuss the topic or hold your hand through a manual solution, your tool will provide—or at least streamline—the end result.

Before you or your team dive into code, it's important to consider other options. There are at least three ways to execute the tool-as-marketing strategy:

- Build it
- Buy it
- Sponsor it

All three of these were present in the Runscope playbook. While they certainly built their own, the most successful projects already existed. A developer's approach is typically to start something new, but often it's best to look for someone who has already done it better. That's a message every developer company shares in their "build vs. buy" communications, yet it's easy to forget when it comes to your own projects.

As you brainstorm ideas for your developer tool, search to see what else already exists. Often, you'll find projects left behind by independent developers. You may even be able to acquire it with the promise to maintain it. Keeping a project going is tough, especially when it was started to scratch an itch or simply for fun. Even if there's only a little traction in a tool, it'll give you a boost you'd otherwise have to bootstrap.

You may find the owner of an existing tool knows that it's worth something. In that case, be prepared to make an offer. As you weigh what it's worth, keep in mind what it would take to rebuild—the tool itself and the traction it's already gained. It's easy to forget the value of your team's time and attention on other projects when determining the price for something that's already built.

Finally, if the price is higher than you're comfortable paying to acquire, you can consider sponsorship. There's not much different about this patron route, as long as you can negotiate the same things you'd include if you owned the property. For example, you want a link to your site and a little message that helps tie the tool to your product. You may also want a tracking pixel for retargeting. It's unlikely you'll want much more, given that part of what helps these tools succeed is their perceived independence.

⅂

On that note, here are two rules, in addition to the three from the previous section, to get the most out of your developer tool:

1. Give it its own home
2. Keep it relevant to your product

It can be tempting to include your new tool (either built or bought) on your existing site. You may be able to get away with it if there are many existing links. However, it will be much harder to get links and shares under the umbrella of your own site. The marketing alignment will be too obvious, and developers feel like their friends could be tricked into your funnel. Plus, the singular focus of a tool is diminished when surrounded by your navigation to the rest of your site.

The second of these new rules may be obvious, but I think it's worth stating explicitly. The problem your tool solves should be as close to one that your product tackles. Your product provides a full-featured solution that takes into account edge cases and company needs. The free tool version is much simpler, but likely is enough for 80% of the developers who find it.

API Transformer is a great example of a tool that solves a focused, important problem. With many different API description formats and versions, developers sometimes need to convert between them before they can use the right tools. APIMatic, the company behind the tool, helps developers turn API descriptions into powerful client libraries, developer portals, and documentation. It shared one small piece of functionality, its ability to convert between formats. Many developers will use the converted document with their own tooling, but a percentage likely stick around to see what's possible with APIMatic.

Another API tool, Postman, started out as a simple Chrome extension. The company is now valued at $2 billion based on its 2020 Series C funding. While no longer attached to Chrome, Postman has kept the same free functionality, which allows developers to try out API requests. Its product is robust, breaking the "do one thing well" rule.

However, the company has added monitors, mock servers, and other features over time. The core initial experience of testing API requests remains. It's likely that almost every Postman user can casually use the free version. But the company can make a big business off the small percentage that need to upgrade features.

You could get the same marketing benefits from your developer tool. Make it free, easy to use, and relevant to your product. Then simply let visitors know that a next step exists if they need it.

ADVERTISING AND SPONSORSHIPS
Enter into Long-Term Partnerships, Not Quick Growth Tactics

While the title puts it solidly in holiday territory, *A Christmas Story* is a movie with lessons applicable all year round. The tale of Ralphie, a kid in the 1950s, is interspersed with his ritual of listening to his favorite radio show. It's within this experience that we can all learn a bit about developer marketing.

The radio show touts a secret decoder ring, available by post. Every day Ralphie checks his mailbox, to no avail. When we finally see the package addressed to him, we can feel his excitement. He listens to the show with anticipation of a series of codes. After writing it down, he runs up to the bathroom, the one place where can be alone. Carefully, Ralphie decodes the numbers into the secret message:

BE SURE TO DRINK YOUR OVALTINE

The letdown is palpable. Both Ralphie and the movie audience were hoping for something more than, in his words, "a crummy commercial."

With experiences like this all around us, developers put up their guard. It is the job of a developer, after all, to anticipate risks and mitigate against them. Naturally, they live their lives much like Ralphie must have after his secret decoder experience: looking out for the tricky advertising.

And yet, it is often the job of a marketer to buy access to an audience. It's typically faster than other channels, but raises developer skepticism. Your challenge is to navigate this dollars-for-eyeballs trade while maintaining developer authenticity.

It's possible to use this channel without spilling your malted milk.

Sponsorships Should Be Partnerships

Once you understand the type of developer you want to reach, it's very likely somebody else is already talking to them. There are likely multiple publications, communities, or tools that attract the right developers for your product. Look for ways to partner with these properties in a way to get your developer tool some authentic attention.

The most common arrangement is to negotiate a one-time or monthly fee in exchange for promotion. Unlike more traditional advertising, almost every aspect of sponsorships can be customized. From dollar amounts to how your message is presented, you can co-create something that works for you, the other party, and—most importantly—that party's audience.

In many cases, you could be the first to approach someone with an offer. Find out what they want from the project you're looking to sponsor. You can expect to spend money, of course, but you might be surprised at what they need. The server bill might be annoying them every month, so simply covering it could remove the stress and keep them focused on the project. After all, nobody likes to see their labors of love bleeding money from their checking account.

When you approach sponsors as partners, rather than as a place to pour advertising dollars, you will do better in the long run. And it's important to consider sponsorships something that will take a while to see the sort of results you may be tempted to measure immediately. You're buying more than the attention of developers. You're also renting the reputation of the person or brand you sponsor. When you truly partner with them, you give the best chance to earn some of that trust with the audience.

Of course, some communities already have sponsors. They may even have defined sponsorship packages. While you'll have less room to define how you pay and what you receive, the partnership approach should be the same. In fact, it may be easier, because there will be clear examples of what has worked before—and what has tanked. The sponsorship opportunities worth taking will be upfront about the best approach and will even help you hone your message.

You should insist that your sponsorship is explicitly stated. You might think you'll get more results from something that looks like editorial coverage. It's true that developers are less skeptical of a message free of bias. However, they'll be most skeptical of a sponsorship that isn't disclosed, and you don't want to be burned by lack of transparency. It's not that developers are particularly serious about journalistic standards—they don't want to be tricked by a crummy commercial.

Among the places you might consider for sponsorship:

- Independent developer tools
- Blogs covering specific technologies

- Email newsletters on relevant topics
- Individual developer influencers
- Events with a technical audience
- Podcasts that discuss developer subjects
- Popular developer YouTube channels
- Anyone with authentic access to the right developers

Developers support companies that sponsor their favorite communities. Ask existing customers what media they consume and use that as a starting place. Or find non-competitors ranking for your important terms and send off a cold email. Treat the sponsorship like any other important relationship and set yourself up to see results.

Depending on the type of sponsorships you try, you may need to adjust the types of metrics you use. For example, you're unlikely to see an immediate bump from a message on a podcast, but over time you should see new customers mention it. Include some room for qualitative measures—or at least leading metrics—and you'll be more likely to see signs that this authentic approach is working.

Advertise to Expand Your Reach

Your developer marketing program can be greatly impacted by sponsorship. In some cases, the sponsored communities become your best referral sources. Each sponsorship can only extend as far as its audience, which may have you looking for more scalable channels. Many marketers explore advertising to increase the number of developers they reach.

As you've read many times in this book, you will be more successful if you approach developers in a non-promotional way. For advertising that seems counterintuitive, but it largely still holds true. In some ways, you have more flexibility for promotion with advertising, because developers certainly know when there's an ad. On the other hand, the presence of advertising will raise a developer skepticism shield, a warning about what they're viewing.

Rather than dive into the ins and outs of ad buys—of which I'm not an expert and the state of the art is always changing—let's look at some methods you can use to defuse skepticism with your advertising.

Promote Content, Not Landing Pages

There are absolutely times for pure marketing messages. As a marketer, you should be testing different ways to acquire your audience. While landing pages are a classic tactic to get leads, you'll find developers are skeptical of any claims within. However, if you can show them authoritative, helpful content, they may be more open to your message.

Run ads with guide content as the promise. In other words, tap into the same understanding of the developer problem and put it forward in the ad copy, as well as the "landing page" a developer will see after you get the click. You can use the existing guide page, or create a special one for ads (which might help with tracking). Gate the guide, if you must, but the same arguments against that apply for advertising.

Your blog post content can also do double duty as ad targets. Help your most successful posts reach an even wider audience. Many blog posts can be as useful as guides, so you can convert the top posts to this format, or simply point ads toward the original post.

Some marketers will use ads as part of a new post's promotion plan. In addition to organic channels, they'll put some ad budget behind the post. For example, you can promote it in social channels, to get some initial momentum behind the topic. Or take the terms where you hope the new post will rank, and artificially move it to the top with ad spend.

When you promote content, you can still use some of the tactics you might employ with any other landing page:

- Define goals for each visitor
- Provide clear calls to action
- Retarget visitors toward conversion

To increase the trust, you might use related content in your retargeting campaign. Through frequent messages, developers will learn to see you as a helpful resource—exactly what you want to be.

Some topics may be more geared toward immediate conversion. For example, a tutorial that solves a specific problem is likely to encourage a developer signup. You can run ads against the terms used to research the problem, with your content as the result. Just as you likely see conversion to a free or trial account as organic, you should similarly see it with your ads.

In general, the more helpful your advertising experience is, the better. Said another way: the less it seems like an ad, the more comfortable a developer will feel taking the actions you want them to take.

Advertising as Sponsorship

Though advertising and sponsorship are covered in the same chapter, they're very different. With advertising you expect more immediate, trackable results. You pay, you get traffic (and the opportunity to convert it). The exchange is pretty clear and transactional. Sponsorship, on the other hand, is more focused on relationships. There's the partnership with the person or entity you're sponsoring, as well as the community of developers. However, sometimes the line between advertising and sponsorship is less clear.

It can be helpful to take a sponsorship approach with large, community-focused publications made up of many smaller groups. For example, Reddit and StackOverflow have millions of users, but only a subset is relevant to your product. These very targeted communities may be worthy of sponsorship, but to reach them requires advertising.

Part of this distinction may be semantics, but to do well requires the right mental approach and some non-advertising methods. When you see one of these ad channels as a sponsorship, you'll look for alternative metrics. And you'll also make sure you maximize the potential through participation.

No developer community wants to be infiltrated by outsiders peddling their wares. As with other sponsorships, look to have a non-advertising presence in the community. Upvote and comment on other posts, share non-promotional content (maybe not even your own). If you have a developer relations team, this is a good opportunity for collaboration. You can combine paid and organic interactions with the community to authentically amplify your message to developers.

Even in these segmented communities, developers will appreciate your sponsorship approach. Other advertisers rarely show a long-term view and often don't present messages that resonate. As a result, developers have learned not to trust most advertising. While this presents a barrier for you, it's also an opportunity to stand out from those just looking to find a developer wallet.

So, if developers are so touchy, why should you even consider advertising or sponsorship?

Because Building Your Own Audience is Hard

As you wade into advertising and sponsorship, it may seem expensive. As with using developer tools as marketing, it can be useful to compare it to the alternative. When you approach an existing audience, you get to bypass all the things that make building one difficult.

Here's a sampling of what is required to build a developer audience:

1. Discover a topic developers care about
2. Express the topic in a way that attracts attention
3. Expand your own understanding of the topic
4. Continue to find new ways to make the topic interesting

Depending on how important the topic is to your company or product, you may be doing these things in addition to sponsorships and advertising. However, using another audience lets you test whether it works. And it gives you results before you've built your following to the same level.

Plus, the content you create may always be seen as a connection to your company, which is different than a truly independent entity. While it's useful to compare alternatives, you should also acknowledge that a sponsorship is an audience you might never be able to build.

DEVELOPER MARKETING ORGANIZATION
Hire the Right People and Set Reasonable Expectations

"You gotta be nuts. And you're gonna need a crew as nuts as you are."

That line kicks off the *Ocean's Eleven* montage to assemble the only team of misfits that could pull off the caper central to the movie. It's a classic trope of the heist genre. And though developer marketing is a much more legal practice, it similarly requires a unique collection of skills.

If you're reading this book—and this chapter, specifically—you might be the Danny or Debbie Ocean of your crew. Every developer marketing team needs a mastermind who can pull the right people together and jump into specific situations themselves. Just as the details of the job influence which roles are needed, your marketing organization will be a unique challenge. Let's look at some of the skills you'll need and how you might structure the talented people you find to join your team.

Skills of the Developer Marketing Unicorn

Developers are unlike any other audience you'll experience in marketing. You need to understand their situation like you've been there yourself, reflect that back to them, and help them understand the next best step to take. The single individual who can fulfill the roles needed for developer marketing are rare. However, it might not be reasonable to hire a specialist in single skills. Instead, look for people who have aptitude for two or more of the common developer marketer needs.

Writing: The Core Marketer Skill

Most marketers, regardless of specialization, can put some words together nicely. They understand the power of active verbs and descriptive adjectives. With developers, you're dealing with technical concepts, but the non-technical words still matter.

Sometimes a good writer without the coding background can lean a little too heavily on their wordsmithing. Developers appreciate efficiency and accuracy. If fewer words will do, they definitely don't want flowery, hand-wavy prose. They'd rather you state it plainly.

Programming: Write and Share Code

Not every team member will need to write code, but any background in the field certainly helps. And you'll definitely need some team members or collaborators to spend time programming. Not only does this make for more authentic interactions with developers, it also will fill out your content. Tutorials, for example, require someone to write code before they write about the code.

Deep programming experience isn't necessarily a requirement, depending upon your audience. If your team can hack together prototypes and examples, that can help you more quickly try something new with developers. You also could use these coding skills to create tools for marketing purposes or internally to make your team identify their impact.

Storytelling: Connect the Right Dots

Related to writing, storytelling can be more broadly applicable. You can use the skill in blog posts, landing pages, videos, and more. It's more than reciting the important points, it's helping developers understand what it means. Marketing needs to be able to help others see the big picture and why a particular development problem matters.

Journalism backgrounds can help here. Look for someone who can sniff out the story, write the lede, and keep digging for more details. They'll also help you remember the story is rarely within your company or product. Yes, you want it featured, but the tales you tell should be about the people impacted and the problems solved.

Data Analysis: Understand What's Working

Marketing activities generate and consume a lot of data. Ideally everyone on your team can dive in and interpret the results. There are specific skills within data analysis, such as manipulating spreadsheets and aggregating files into a single view. But there are also the softer things, like choosing the right granularity and exploring orthogonal hunches.

Team members who excel in data analysis will need access to every touchpoint in the developer journey. That includes analytics for the marketing website, your portal or docs, and any other property that's important to developers. You'll also want to pull out email logs, GitHub metrics, and maybe even downloads for every package manager. Some of these tools may be owned by other departments, but you'll need access in marketing.

Speaking: Share Your Message Everywhere

Like a good writer, a marketer who can speak in public will amplify their impact to the company and product. Whether it's at physical events, webinars, or with makeshift groups of interested developers, you want a representative who is comfortable with a technical crowd. They're personable, knowledgeable, and able to speak authentically about developer topics.

You don't need to wait for events to invite these speakers. You can organize the events yourself or use recorded videos in place of time-restricted occasions. The team members who are good at speaking are willing to do it a lot. Support them, make sure they don't burn out, and find ways to acknowledge their impact on the team.

Teaching: Educate and Inspire Developers

Related to speaking, developer marketers should approach interactions like an educator. This lens expands beyond speaking situations. Written content should help developers better understand a technical problem and help them to a solution. So should your website itself, onboarding, documentation, and more.

You could say teaching is an important part of all marketing, regardless of whether it's for developers. That would be true and a useful approach for anyone who wants to make an impact. For developer marketers, there's no other way.

Problem-solving: For Yourself and Your Audience

Before you can teach, you need to understand the objectives. That means your team should be good at identifying problems, solving them, and then sharing them with others. You want to be able to identify internal issues—such as how to get the data needed for analysis—but you primarily will be focused on the problems your developers experience.

It can be easy to recommend solutions that are in search of problems. While you want your product (the solution) to be a star in your problem-solving adventures, it's important to remember that it starts with the developer. What is their journey and how can you tap into it?

User Research: Listen to Developers

While research may be a department in some organizations, it's everyone's job to understand your developer users. Especially in marketing, listening will help you solve the right problems that attract attention. Knowing the developer point of view lets you find where it crosses over with your company's opinions, which will allow you to tell the stories you need to grow your community.

There are many ways to apply your team's listening skills: in live interviews, by reading terse feedback comments, and even by analyzing traffic patterns (developer actions—or non-actions—can tell you a lot).

Empathy: Understand Developer Pains

Your team needs to put themselves in the developer's shoes. This can be helpful while performing research, but also throughout your marketing activities. Of course, it's easier to harness empathy if you've lived the coding lifestyle of your audience. But that's not a requirement.

Look for team members who can look outward, rather than inward. The purpose of marketing is to appeal to developers, not to appease internal teams. It does no good to tout your product's features if it does not resonate—empathetically—with the right developers.

The Marketing Organization and Beyond

Now that you know what skills to attract, you can think about where to apply this collection of special abilities. Your organization's structure will determine which roles sit where. Developer marketers must be collaborative in order to be successful, so don't skip past something that is outside your group. You'll need to work with each of these roles, whether they're "on your team," report to someone else, or even work outside your company. Some of Ocean's Eleven were only needed for short, very specific duties. For your dream team, think beyond the job listing.

Content: Reach Developers with Words

A steady supply of content is the lifeblood of developer marketing. It helps you explore new topics and continue the drumbeat of your message. While the written word is the most common—and likely will need to remain a staple of your arsenal—you should consider beyond writing for a complete content team. You might want videos (of various types), podcasts, and other media types within your developer content.

Expect to piece together your content program with contributions from across the company, full-time marketers, and trusted external sources. Someone on your team will need to own the strategy and metrics, though you may partner with an outside expert to confirm your approach.

In addition to content production, think about your process to review, edit, approve, publish, and promote content, as well. Some of these duties may fall within content or collaboration with other team members and departments.

Growth: Move Your Most Important Metrics

In recent years, marketing has created a new role—sometimes its own distinct department—called "growth." Some use it as a synonym for marketing, without any other marketing department. In other cases, it's distinct, but one thing that remains in all incarnations: the desire to see the numbers go in the right direction.

There are many tactics in the growth toolbox, many of which have been discussed in this book. To be most widely applied, growth teams often include the elements needed to build new products. In the most mature organizations, it's common to see growth engineers, designers, and product managers, in addition to the marketer.

Developer Relations: Connect with Your Audience

The soul of a developer company lives in its developer relations team members. Often misunderstood and misused, developer relations plays an important role between your company and the developers you want to attract. In the best organizations, the messages flow both ways—company to developer and developer to company, through the developer relations team.

Sometimes, especially in the early days, you have a team of one. The titles differ, but often are among the following variants:

- Developer Evangelist
- Developer Advocate
- Community Manager
- Developer Relations Director

That last one is a variable and will be dependent on the level of the leader you bring in to start the program. These names can mean slightly different things. Evangelists are typically more outwardly focused on bringing your message to developers. Advocates, by contrast, return to the organization with product feedback, the voice of the developer. Community managers tend to be less technical and aimed at virtual collaboration.

Fig. 14 DevRelOMeter Calculates Developer Advocacy and Developer Evangelism Activities

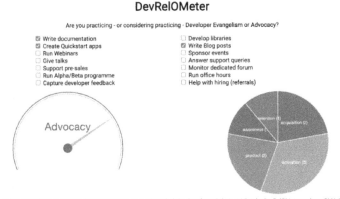

Most importantly, none of these duties or titles is set in stone. The best developer relations pros will use the approach described in this book to educate and inspire the right developers. The best department for developer relations is the one who will support their cause. Most commonly, it is either a part of marketing or product.

Product Marketing: Hone and Amplify Your Message

Depending on the size of your company, you may not have anyone with the product marketing title. Or you could have an entire department. Regardless of what you call it, this hybrid of product and marketing includes important go-to-market activities. A product marketer deeply understands the audience, how the product is used, and prepares the materials needed to share the product with developers.

Product pages, landing pages, industry breakdowns, and use case descriptions are all product marketing work. In some cases, a product marketer will jump in on top-of-funnel content. If your company has sales, product marketing will help provide the materials the team needs to close deals. It's a catch-all role that includes many of the developer marketing skills—possibly even coding at a developer company.

As you might guess, product marketing usually sits in either marketing or product. Either way, this role collaborates with both departments and many more.

Developer Experience: Support the Developer Journey

To meet the broad needs of developer experience (outlined in an earlier chapter), many companies establish entire departments dedicated to the practice. Smaller companies may have one or two people with "developer experience" in their titles, which could include technical writers or engineers. While those are the two most likely roles, the needs within developer experience are wide.

The initial experience is a prime area of focus for this role or department. That means signup, onboarding, and dashboard will be important concerns. Often SDKs are maintained by the developer experience team, which knows the value of helpful libraries. In addition to SDK code, developer experience often requires product tweaks to streamline usage. Lifecycle emails may fall under developer experience, as well, so you can re-engage developers who have started to kick the tires—or who were once engaged but have now disappeared.

Since documentation is a core element of a developer's experience with a technical product, it is often part of developer experience.

However, some organizations split it out. Indeed, developer experience is sometimes a subset of a documentation team. Or it can be an umbrella which also includes developer relations and other developer-focused departments.

Documentation: Share Accurate and Updated Information

You may not think of documentation as marketing, but you should. When developers are your audience, they'll use your documentation to answer important questions about your product. Does your API do what they expect? How do they get started? These questions overlap considerably with developer experience. One useful way to separate the two (if that's necessary) is that documentation provides the factual content, while developer experience brings the context.

It's unlikely that documentation is part of the marketing organization, despite being an important element. You will often collaborate with the documentation team and reference its work. Potentially, marketing will contribute use case and tutorial content, though that may also live in another location.

Internal Collaborators: Subject Matter Experts

Many more roles overlap with developer marketing needs. While unlikely to be part of a marketing organization, these will surely be important collaborators:

- API Product Manager
- Customer Support
- Technical Account Managers

- Sales Engineers
- Solutions Engineers
- Customer Success

You might go to these roles and departments for a better understanding of the audience or as content contributors. Each has its specialization and often much of their knowledge is not shared publicly. Where customer privacy is not required, marketing can help amplify important developer stories from these other areas of the company.

External Collaborators: Specific Skills Beyond the Team

Similarly, you won't always have enough bandwidth or background on the team to tackle certain developer marketing projects. That's where you might collaborate with these external agencies and individuals:

- Search engine optimization
- Link building
- Developer strategy
- Content writing
- Advertising
- Conversion optimization
- Podcast or video editing

That's an incomplete list, but you can expand your abilities when you find targeted and talented external collaborators. In some cases, you may be filling gaps in knowledge or due to a delay in hiring the right person. In other cases, it may simply be to scale capacity. Most developer marketing teams seem to operate with fewer people than they'd ideally need. Using outside talent can be an effective way to get more done with less.

Set the Right Expectations of Each Role

When I was the editor of ProgrammableWeb, which was called the journal of the API economy, I attended a lot of conferences. Sometimes I would speak about API trends, but often my goal was to meet representatives from API companies. It wasn't your typical networking, because I had nothing to sell and wasn't a typical buyer. To learn more about a company with the potential for future coverage, we'd usually exchange business cards. Periodically, after a week or so, I would get automated sales emails from a company, usually not the person I met. I could look back at my pile of cards and, at least inside my head, write a negative story about their API strategy.

These sorts of email campaigns aren't always a bad idea, though they don't usually resonate with a developer audience. Absent the context of the conversation that took place, they won't be very effective. The worst offense this strategy uncovers is someone has the wrong expectations for a role. In an effort to track results and prove your position, you can erode the very trust you're looking to build with developers.

You should not expect immediate conversions from attending developer events. Beware of how blindly you track leads from certain events, because that may very well cause tone-deaf follow-ups. Allow your teams that work with developer communities to do their best work. Explore methods that will resonate, then your great developer experience can complete the conversion.

Developer relations and documentation should not be expected to directly convert users.

Blatant calls to action within an API reference will either be ignored or negatively called out. Worse, it could be seen as a trick that raises that skepticism you've worked so hard to diminish.

Even content is difficult to track by conversion. Many times, the posts that attract initial attention aren't the ones that get a signup. You can find fancy tools to distribute attribution, but it won't catch everything in this multi-device, cookie-blocking world. By all means, continue to instrument your systems, but don't hold content to an expectation it can't meet. Instead, look at traffic patterns and whether topics match your developer's needs.

The more traditional the role within marketing, the more likely you'll be able to use common expectations. But there are few of those roles in developer marketing, where you must keep the developer audience in mind at every step.

CONCLUSION
Do This Next

Gower Champion didn't know anything about developer marketing. In fact, the legendary Broadway director died in 1980. You'd be shocked, then, to get advice from him that you can apply to your job. It turns out, this master of the stage still has relevant words for all of us.

The story goes that one day the director walked into a rehearsal to find everyone sitting around. They were at a creative impasse. Surely the Great Gower Champion and his eight Tony Awards could lend some inspiration.

Instead, Champion turned to his choreographer and said:

"Do something, so we can change it."

Before you close this book, choose one thing to try in your developer marketing. It doesn't matter that you select the right thing, only that you take some action. The simple act of "doing something" can help you see what needs to change.

Throughout this book, you've learned about EveryDeveloper's approach to technical audiences. You've seen how, regardless of the channel, you need to understand and address developer problems. You should seek to educate and inspire, not promote. Teach developers something new and you will earn their trust.

Developer marketing does not exist because you can't bring your typical tactics to this skeptical audience. If you use regular marketing with developers, it will fall flat. At best, you'll be ignored. At worst, developers will ridicule your company. You want every message to resonate. Even product announcements should feel developer-focused, not you-focused. To achieve this, in all that you do: share knowledge, not features.

When there are many potential actions to take, it's natural to feel paralyzed. To help, browse the following suggestions, one for each chapter:

Developer Experience

Prepare an environment where developers will thrive.

☐ Assess your developer portal on the 13 elements of developer experience, then improve one of them today.

Blog Posts

Reach more developers with frequent, helpful articles

☐ Look up your most popular posts by traffic, then create three headlines for potential posts you can write that are similar.

Tutorials

Teach developers exactly how to solve their problems

☐ Make sure you have tutorials for your three most common use cases, with code in your three most popular programming languages. That's nine tutorials—can you collect them all?

Guides

Show how deeply you understand what a developer needs

☐ Brainstorm a list of potential keywords you'd own if you could, then narrow them to a single topic, so you can begin outlining your Signature Content.

Events

Meet developers where they are with authentic interactions

☐ Select an upcoming event (either scheduled or not) and discuss engagement ideas with two other team members, including one from outside marketing.

Open Source and Community

Listen and contribute to a broader group of developers

☐ Take stock of existing open source repositories, including open issues and pull requests from outside your company. Who needs to address these?

Tools as Marketing

Build something the right developers will want to use

☐ Choose one small feature of your product and try to find an existing free tool that solves the same problem. Could you acquire, sponsor, or reproduce that tool?

Advertising and Sponsorships

Enter into long-term partnerships, not quick growth tactics

☐ Find someone already interacting with the right developers and explore partnership opportunities. It doesn't necessarily have to cost a lot.

Developer Marketing Organization

Hire the right people and set reasonable expectations

☐ Review your marketing metrics and flag any that might make it difficult to reach developers authentically. What could you track instead?

Need Developer Marketing Guidance?

Strangely, it is most difficult to see the things that are in front of you every day. Sometimes all that's required is a pair of fresh eyes. You can work with the EveryDeveloper team to uncover the high priority projects for your developer marketing team to tackle.

Or work with our team of talented writers to deliver new content to your technical audience.

Find out more at **everydeveloper.com**

Acknowledgements

This book is more than a decade in the making, inspired by all my colleagues, collaborators, and clients too numerous to mention.

During the month I set aside to write the first draft, my family watched me make a cup of coffee and venture out to the office for several hours, seven days a week. Thank you, Jenny, Evan, Alana, and Isabel. I love you!

The EveryDeveloper team stepped up to support in big and small ways. In particular, I am grateful for Holly Walsh, Luke Russell, Betsy Clayton, and Kirill Satanovsky.

Thanks to John Musser for seeking me out and trusting me with ProgrammableWeb. I appreciate your continued friendship and guidance.

To make this book a whole lot better, Pam Greer provided fantastic development feedback and copy edits. She also kept things moving when they could have slowed. Similarly, I tip my cap to Brian Schwartz for the on-call publishing expertise that saved me time.

Everybody needs a sounding board. I can always count on Kai Davis, Connie Whitesell, and Alex Theis. You amplified my voice when I was uncertain.

Finally, thank you to early readers, reviewers, and reassurers. You cauhgt everry mitsake!

Adam DuVander

Access the
Developer Marketing Library

Get the most out of this book—and your developer marketing. Your purchase of *Developer Marketing Does Not Exist* gains you access to a library full of Developer Marketing resources that will help grow and connect with developers on their terms.

You want to attract, engage, inspire, and educate developers?

The *Developer Marketing Library* provides you with:

- Worksheets for audience clarity
- Checklists for content development
- Templates for well-structured technical content

Plus other tools to reach more developers.

Visit **everydeveloper.com/library**

About the Author

Adam DuVander is a former developer, accidental marketer, and founder of EveryDeveloper. He's worked with some of the best developer-focused companies as an early employee, team leader, and consultant. Many seek his advice on content strategy, developer experience, and community engagement. An API veteran, he previously served as the first editor of ProgrammableWeb, wrote a book on mapping APIs, and covered developer topics for Wired. He lives with his family in Portland, Oregon.

About EveryDeveloper

When you want to reach more of the right developers, you need to educate and inspire them with great technical content. EveryDeveloper has helped dozens of developer-focused companies attract millions of developers to their products. Services include developer marketer training, developer experience reviews, and technical content strategy. Find out more at **everydeveloper.com**